Where Is Somebody?

Bullen Dolli Timo

Acknowledgments

The Author, Bullen Dolli Timo, wishes to express his gratitude to the following people: Pastor Y. J. Timo (his late, beloved grandfather, Lisa Mitchell (his American mother and assistant editor), George Yeager (who motivated him to write this book), Mrs. Jane Morson for her excellent help in finding a publisher, The entire Morson Family (good friends for many years), and lastly but always first in his heart, Jesus Christ, son of the living God, for whom we owe all our successes.

Where is Somebody?

Table of Contents

Chapter 1:   Retreat   11
Chapter 2:   I Was Born   17
Chapter 3:   Civil War   23
Chapter 4:   Moving On With Life   31
Chapter 5:   Next Generation   47
Chapter 6:   Displaced Camp   57
Chapter 7:   Missionary Impact   63
Chapter 8:   Search Is On   73
Chapter 9:   USA Adventure   85
Chapter 10: More Studies   95
Chapter 11: Faith and Family   113
Chapter 12: Associates to Bachelors   123
Chapter 13: Returning as a Missionary   129
Chapter 14: Appreciation   139

CHAPTER ONE - RETREAT

How can this God story be celebrated? I was told a prize would be given. I had never won anything. My mind was spinning a million times. What is the prize? There I was, a young Sudanese man, at an international student's conference, where hundreds gathered for a night of food and fun, and to meet other students from around the world.

The meeting began like many others do, with students and other guests greeting one another. I became comfortable when I came face-to-face with fellow Africans from Rwanda, a neighboring country. We spent time chatting and connecting over things only we "Africans" might understand. It wasn't until later that others would get a glimpse of the life we had once lived.

I found a seat next to my new Rwandan friend. I honestly had no anticipation of winning, simply because I never thought I would be able to answer any questions correctly. The event coordinator, a kind lady, stepped to the microphone and told us to stand up if the answer to the questions she was about to ask were yes. She encouraged all of us to participate and to look around as the questions were answered.

"Have you ever spent the night at an airport?" and at that almost every single person in the room stood up.

"Has anyone in this room ever been on television?" and I stood up with other students, but the number of people standing was definitely smaller.

"Who here has been affected by a civil war?" My new Rwandan friend and I both stood to our feet, and as we looked around, we were alone.

My mind is now thinking, "I might be able to win this prize. What in the world would the next question be?"

"Who was born in their house and not at the hospital?" Silence was in the room and every person's eyes were looking around to see who would stand next.

I slowly stood to my feet and glanced in all directions to see that I was the last man standing. The lady walked close to my seat; then she repeated the question.

"You were born in your house?" And I replied, "Yes ma'am, I was born in a mud hut in Mundri, South Sudan." Some of the audience perhaps thought that my mother chose to deliver me at home, but what they did not know was, she had no choice.

And then she asked why, and I explained that Sudanese ladies delivered their babies in their homes because there were no hospitals within even hours of our homes.

"You must be joking," the lady said. So I replied, "No joke ma'am, this is life in the depths of South Sudan," and with that final remark I had won, I won, I won the prize. It was a t-shirt which was too large for me, and a frisbee which I had no idea how to use (not that I was ungrateful for them).

This kind of story about my being born on a dirt floor of a tukul because there was no hospital, is all true. But more unbelievable is the fact that I witnessed a civil war that took more than a million lives, where thousands of people were forced to leave their villages and some of them walked hundreds of miles, running for their lives. How can it even be possible for anyone to be curious about these stories? What is the benefit or gain of telling about this life I've lived?

Only one thing, and that is that there is God's grace, goodness, protection, and mercy in my life. If this were not His story, then I would not be giving any testimony at all.

Dad and Mom

My dad, Bennett, married my mom, Mary, at a very young age. This is common in my country because there is no such thing as school past the 6th grade. Boys and girls get through their early teens and it is time to get married.

When Sudan gained its independence from Britain in 1956, the Muslims, in the North, took charge. They began to control and exploit the people in the South in the largest country in Africa. Our entire culture changed at this point including education and social status because of our religious differences. So many people lost their lives as a result of their belief in Jesus Christ. My father did not get to finish his studies because Christians were forced to quit school unless they renounced their faith.

Bennett spent his entire life in the bush, or deep jungle. He was born in the bush, grew up in the bush, and all he ever knew was war and people trying to escape death and hoping for peace. Bennett learned from his father, Yerobama, all the skills he needed to take care of his family. My dad loved people and was a man of many friends. He longed for all people to get along, regardless of their religious beliefs, or nationality. My father befriended peoples from any tribe. The family unit is so important and I know my father and grandfather were so proud of their families.

On the other side, Mary was the first-born child and she has three sisters and nine brothers. My sweet mom did not get to attend school at all; instead, she stayed home to help her mother in raising such a large family. Mary already knew how to be a good wife and mother before she started having her own children. She worked hard to teach what she learned from her mother to her daughter. Mary and Bennett's family was large before I was born. I have five brothers and only one sister. My eldest brother's name is Elijah, followed by Abetere, Jabi, Wani, and Lumari, and then, my sister, Florence Kamala.

General Customs

There is so much dignity in tribal customs. Knowing these helps others understand my story a little better. The sixty-four tribes in South Sudan have their own language. Speaking and writing the tribal language is mandatory and is taught by family. Any interaction with someone from my tribe, or from my family requires my tribal language.

My language is called Moru and the pronunciation of most of the words end in a vowel sound. For example, the name Beth would be pronounced "Betty" and the name Jan would be pronounced "Janie". South Sudanese people also have to learn Arabic which allows us to communicate and link all the different tribal groups in the country.

Some tribes cut designs in their foreheads or faces to identify themselves from other tribes. My mother and my grandfather have a cut identification in the temple area on their faces. This custom was not being followed when I was born, thank goodness.

When dressing for a special occasion, men often may wear what appears to be a dress. It really is a robe-type garment.

Out of respect for each other, a Moru daughter-in-law is not supposed to eat with the parents of her husband for some time. The same custom is applied for the son in-law to his wife's parents. Marriages have to be confirmed by all members of the family (on both sides), with a family representative, usually a distant cousin, passing on the decisions. The groom must pay a dowry to the bride's family and this payment may take years to complete.

When a family member or a friend passes away, the entire community jumps into action. The family does not sleep until the body is in the ground. A hole is dug near the home, and a box (casket) is constructed out of teak wood, and the body is wrapped tightly in a bed sheet. If possible, the body is taken to a nearby church where prayers, singing, and mourning take place. The community helps to bury the body and stones are collected to cover the site. Sometimes the family will purchase cement and cover the top of the burial place to resemble a tomb.

CHAPTER TWO - I WAS BORN

It is February in the remote town of Mundri, South Sudan and the heat is brutal. Temperatures can rise to 100 or more degrees during the day and the evenings are not much cooler. Grasses are brown and scorched, our water holes are dried up, and fires start burning in the middle of nowhere. Strong dust bowls swirl through the air and conditions are just terrible. At the same time, it is time for hunting, fishing, and harvesting honey for the men, and the women slow down waiting on the rainy season. The biggest challenge at this time of the year is finding water.

My small-framed momma, who is spunky, walked several miles to draw water before the sun came up on February 9, 1985, and little did she know that I would be arriving that morning. Our community is small with no clinic, no midwife, and no doctor, not even a nurse in the whole village. My mom called for all the older women in the area to come and help as labor began. Newborn babies in South Sudan are more likely to die in the first 24 hours of life because of the difficult conditions.

Inside the thatch grass covered room in the middle of the jungle, I was born. My mother's clothes were used for wrapping me as I entered the world. On the dirt floor, my mom laid me on a coconut mat giving thanks to our Heavenly Father for her seventh blessing, depending on God for my survival. I started my journey on earth this day in the cone-shaped mud hut, and God protected me.

Naming the Child

In my Moru tribe, the entire family takes part in the naming of a new little one. A name always has a meaning, which might be selected from a visitor in the village, a deceased family member or a community leader with great influence.

Upon my arrival, volunteers walked miles and miles to tell extended family members of the happy event. Everyone began to travel for the celebration of my new life. This is kind of like a family reunion with gifts. The elder women began preparing available food for the guests. Coffee and tea was brewed for days. After three days, the pastor and the family came together for a meal and thanksgiving prayers just for me. Many gifts were brought in my honor, one being a customary animal (deer) skin back wrap.

During this festivity, my name was carefully discussed and chosen. I was named Bullen Dolli Jangara Timo. My name Bullen was chosen from an English missionary by this name. He traveled to South Sudan in the 1940s and died here while serving the Lord. My grandfather, a pastor, knew him and his passion for Christ.

My Sudanese name, Dolli, was also the name of a distant uncle, who was an influential man in the village of Lui. He was a funny man with great compassion for other people.

The name Jangara is the middle (Sudanese) name of my grandfather (father's father), and Timo is my father's family name.

God knew my name before I was born, and He was and is, and will be sovereign over even the little details.

Many of the customs in South Sudan can be very confusing for the western world but also very interesting. As a toddler when my teeth began to come in, another Moru custom took place. There was a strong belief, due to limited knowledge and understanding that the swelling on the gums in the area of the eyeteeth was the cause of persistent fever and diarrhea. A man in our village, who was a traditional healer, known as the tooth puller, would come to our house to perform the extractions. This practice of digging, or cutting out of the tooth buds in a child was his way of making a living. The sharp instrument used for this procedure could be a hot needle, a blade made from a spoon handle, or possibly a bike spoke. He would use whatever was available to cut through the gum and you know that there was no such thing as sterilization or numbing medicine.

This crazy custom created so many future dental problems. For me, it caused a large space between my two front teeth and caused my teeth to grow in many different directions. My Orthodontist, Dr. Jana Roberts, was so shocked at my dental x-rays. The buds of my bottom eyeteeth were not fully removed and the calcium pod was killing the roots of the teeth. I could not have braces put on my bottom teeth for fear of them falling out while being moved. I guess I will have false or no teeth at all in my old age. As time evolves, some customs have been banished while others still exist. Life in the bush still goes on as customs are passed from generation to generation.

As I began to crawl, walk, and grow, I feel I must have played with my siblings and other children though that memory is vague at the very best. I can only imagine how happy my parents were with their precious family. I am so proud and thankful for my beloved mom and dad. I will be forever honored of where I was born. God chose me to be born in the land of Africa, with all its beauty and wildness. A land filled with the majesty of God's creation, such as mountains and jungles, raging rivers, small streams...tall elephant grass and thick vegetation, barren land and dusty dirt, too, along with wild animals, singing birds, and an abundance of rain and dry skies for months, thunder and lighting so beautiful in the darkest of nights.

I saw and learned about many different tribes of native South Sudan. God also chose me to live off this land, to eat roots and leaves during starvation, and to have no clean water for drinking, and to fight the heat and disease. Malaria was the number one killer in Africa throughout my childhood and it is

Chapter Two - I Was Born

still raging today throughout my country. All of the extreme changes in the environment come with the blessings of each season.

After reading through this chapter you may be thinking, "What on earth!!" I am always excited because this life is not about how it started, but about how it's going to finish. Many people that I have met tend to focus on what has happened in the past instead of focusing on what lies ahead of them. I will forever be filled with joy that God's hand was on me when I was born and I know His hand will be with me in the end. I want to encourage each of you to seek great things in your future. We have a future that is not determined by our past or where we were born. The greatest joy of facing all the odds in this life is to know the One who holds the future. Life is a long journey, and it begins with your entrance on earth and it will stop when you exit this life. It will be your choice on how you walk this road.

> *"For You formed my inward parts; You wove me in my mother's womb. I will give thanks to You, for I am fearfully and wonderfully made; Wonderful are Your works, And my soul knows it very well. My frame was not hidden from You, when I was made in secret, and skillfully wrought in the depths of the earth; Your eyes have seen my unformed substance; And in Your book were all written the days that were ordained for me, when as yet there was not one of them."*
>
> **Psalms 139:13-16**

Chapter Three - Civil War

Can you believe that nine different countries touch Sudan? It is bordered by Uganda in the South, Kenya and Ethiopia to the East, Eretria, Egypt, and Libya are to the north, Chad and the Central African Republic is in the west and finally the Democratic Republic of Congo. All these countries watched Sudan at war with itself, in a battle with its own people for decades. 'Sharia' or Islamic law governs not only religious rituals, but also all aspects of day-to-day life and was already part of the system at this time. It does not favor Christians at all. People live in fear; random villages are raided and each human is taken captive or killed.

Being born during the longest civil war in Africa, I thought this was the life that everyone was living all over the world. I had no idea what it meant to be free or living in freedom.

My days were filled with playing in and around my family compound, and performing chores. You know each one of us has our own age appropriate responsibilities to be done daily while living off the land, but at this particular time my full time job was being a kid. My big brothers had to gather firewood for the evening. They had to sweep the dirt area in and around our tukuls with large pieces of elephant grass or branches of trees tied together, kind of like a broom. This helped to clear the places where scorpions and snakes like to hide.

South Sudan is near the equator in an area of the world known as Western Equatoria and it became dark at nearly the same time every single day of the year. As darkness fell each evening, my family prayed to thank God for the food that had been prepared by the women and for God's protection during the night. Then after one horrifying evening everything would change forever, and no one suspected that this would be the last time we would pray together as a family.

Root of Conflict

The civil war between Muslim forces of the Khartoum government and the Sudanese People's Liberation Army (SPLA in the south) was now not just a war in other parts of the country but was happening right in front of me. My parents must have been aware of the presence of the SPLA positioning for a counter attack because the school had closed for my older siblings. I am sure my mom was nervous and there were conversations among the adults that we could be in danger, but from my standpoint I was just living in the moment, playing like there was no tomorrow.

The Muslims showed up to take everyone in the village; the goal was to take everyone as a prisoner or slave and burn anything that remained in their path. This strategy would wipe out everything and even if someone escaped from this attack there would be nothing left for him or her to survive. However, they did not fully succeed. God had greater plans for us, and at the age of four, I survived! I don't remember much before the raid because I was so little; but I do know the time was morning. I was playing about three miles outside of Mundri at my grandmother's village. The ground shook as weapon shells rained down and everyone was running in circles. The sounds were so loud my insides vibrated and my eyes and heart knew something really bad was taking place, but I had no idea of the magnitude. We encountered one of the biggest devastations in the history of our lives.

Village Seized

On this terrible day my mom, dad, brothers and sister were taken as prisoners and unbeknownst to me at the time, I would not hear about them or see them for many years. As the bombs exploded all around, people dropped what they were doing and ran for the bush area to hide from the attack. It was the rainy season and the area was thick with tall grasses growing between big trees with no open paths. Someone from my grandmother's village grabbed my hand and we ran and stumbled through smoke and fire. I heard screams and cries of the wounded and captives and saw people pleading for help. It was complete turmoil and many tukuls (homes) were burning with fire bigger than I had ever seen. I had no shoes and was dressed in the shirt and shorts that I wore to bed. I wish I had changed my clothes when I woke up because this would be my only garments for the next several years.

We continued to run deeper and deeper into the jungle for what seemed like forever. I had never run so hard in my whole life and shells were still falling in the bush where we were looking for shelter from this chaos. Moving as fast as my little legs would take me, yet being pulled by my arm attached to an adult, my chest hurt and tears streamed down my face. I struggled to catch my breath in the dense brush. In moments of resting and standing still, I remember glancing around looking for my family; I wanted to see my mom, dad, or at least one of my older brothers. I only caught glimpses of other people running in the same general direction. We ran mile after mile to the south of Mundri and gradually the sound of fighting and explosions grew farther away.

Chapter Three - Civil War

My grandmother, Penina (mother of my mother), and I ended up in a place called Nyau, about 15 miles from where we started this journey. Exhausted, hot and hungry, I sat quietly with the other refugees whose numbers grew by the minute. However, no members of my immediate family showed up. I was too immature to think about whether or not they had survived and I would not know the answer to that question until much later.

The days that followed this adventure to Nyau were very cloudy for me. I struggle now to know whether I want to remember them or if I was actually too little to recall what really happened during those dreadful weeks. The beautiful life with a mom, dad, brothers, and sister had changed forever in the blink of an eye. I survived not because I am fast or clever, but God rescued me and He ran with me every step of the way!

My parental grandfather was a traveling preacher or evangelist. He was in a remote village about 10 miles away sharing the gospel at a revival conference when this attack took place. As he walked home and entered the clearing where our compound once stood, ashes and destruction told him the story. He began the search for his family moving towards the south of Mundri. Nyau was the direction and place where, as a child, he once hid from Muslims. Days later, he found me with grandmother, Penina.

Here comes another Moru custom: younger siblings and direct descendant children or grandchildren are the responsibility of the oldest living male in the family. Therefore, I was supposed to go with Baba, and I did. From this day forward, life was my

Baba and I in the dense jungle of South Sudan. As I look back, this was kind of a starting over. Although, we had very little in our Mundri compound, we had just the clothes on our back in Nyau.

There was no land cleared, no shelter, no garden, no water, no hand tools, no shoes, no mom, no dad, no brothers or sister; Absolutely Nothing! I remember Baba returning all those miles to my original home to collect what he could salvage. I can still see clearly my Baba holding his bow in his left hand with his quiver on his shoulder as he walked towards Mundri. The only item I recall that he found was an ax, and he told me, "This is all we have." Baba would bring items to Nyau, a little at a time, as he would travel to preach and return. One thing that God provided for my aching heart was my Baba. He was all I had on earth. For the next 14 years he and I lived life together on little more than the roots of wild fruit, but God provided everything we needed to survive.

My pre-school life was so painful that recalling all the hunger, gunfire, and the unknown made me sad and brought fear to my heart. I was able to still visit Penina, from time to time, as Baba's schedule allowed. Of course, I can see this now, but then I really didn't understand that life was so tough and that everyone was simply trying to stay alive. I am sure my grandfather leaned on the Lord to help us through each and every day. This plan of destroying all of us in the village did not work well. Some of us escaped alive because God had different plans for our lives. Many situations came into our lives but they were just for a season.

It is summer today, but soon it will be fall and then winter, and then spring will follow and chase us all the way back to summer again. In every season of life, God is faithful and He will be forever. All that you need to make it through; His hand will provide. Trust in His greatness.

"For I know the plans that I have for you," declares the Lord, "plans for welfare and not for calamity to give you a future and a hope."

Jeremiah 29:11

Chapter Four - Moving On With Life

During the first few years in Nyau, I grew up really fast. Life was simple, friendly, and full of thankfulness, but can I tell you it was also adventurous, scary, and difficult. I was a very tiny small-framed boy, who learned great lessons from a wise grandfather, to whom I will be forever grateful.

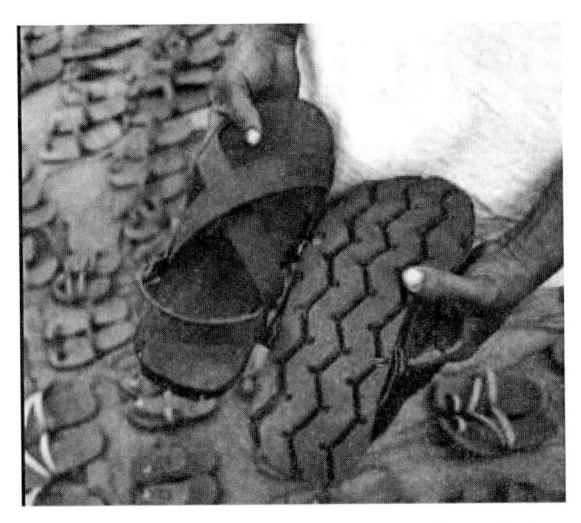

I had no shoes, so one time when Baba returned from preaching he brought back a pair for me. The shoes were made from an old rubber tire and were so heavy and sturdy. My feet were very protected, but I could barely keep them on my feet with the giant wide straps over the top. I know for sure I did not wear these shoes out, but I do not recall when or where they left my wardrobe.

In our culture, ladies are the ones to fetch the water, care for the children, weed and harvest the crops, and cook all the meals for the family. With no mom, I dug the garden with a hoe bigger than myself until my little legs felt weak.

I walked miles for water with an empty can to collect water for whoever was caring for me at the time. Our nearest water source was a hole in the ground 2 to 3 miles away. Getting water was not an easy chore and it was so heavy to carry back home. I really missed having a momma; there were so many things I needed to tell her.

Looking back, I never had a childhood where I was able to just be a kid. I have seen how children live in the States; carefree, no responsibilities, playing with so many toys and games, eating healthy fruits and vegetables, writing with colorful markers on white paper, and swinging on playgrounds made just for them. I don't even know what that would be like, but God loved me so much just to keep me alive and I am so thankful. I slept in the dirt, contracted malaria, had one set of clothing, listened for incoming aircraft dropping bombs, hid in foxholes, worshipped the Almighty God, was bullied by friends, lived with baboons and hyenas, and I was bitten by ... keep reading, I will tell you later.

In the jungle, we lived life the best that we

Chapter Four - Moving On With Life

could. As days turn to weeks, to months, to years, tukuls were built for shelter, gardens were planted for food, wood was gathered for fire. The gathering of firewood for warmth, cooking, and light was a daily requirement in the bush. Although trees were standing everywhere I looked, the collection of branches for our fire must have fallen to the ground. The sound of a tree falling in the woods was music to my ears, as it meant the task of gathering firewood would be easier the following day.

One of the most important life lessons growing up was to know how to build a shelter over my head. Using an ax or machete, hundreds of small trees and bamboo shoots must be cut. It could take days to chop, drag, and gather enough bamboo to make a hut. The fresh poles have to dry while you start cutting, bundling, and then carrying the elephant grass on your head. South Sudan is blessed with an abundance of elephant grass. After all material is gathered and the land is cleared, it is time to build your dream tukul. Holes are dug, poles are placed and woven together, mud is mixed and smeared into the cracks, and the roof is made like a cone with more poles and tied together, grasses are piled high to complete the roof. Elephant grass is also piled inside to make a bed and a coconut mat is placed on top to lie on. The doors are made out of grass or straw, but we build them after the tukul is finished. This process takes about 2 months to finish and then you are ready to invite all of your neighbors for the thanksgiving prayers. Each home is prayed over and God is praised for helping you in the whole process of building your new house.

Chapter Four - Moving On With Life

Tukuls are not very big places, so in a compound you have several of them built kind of in a circle or a little distance from each other. Babies are always with their mama until about 5 years, so they sleep on the same straw mat with them. Male and female children have separate tukuls. Sometimes a kitchen tukul is built for cooking and another one for storage. A tukul does not have a bathroom. Two deep holes are dug in the ground a little distance away from your tukul and they usually have some tall bamboo sticks staked in the ground around them for privacy, kind of like an outhouse without a seat. One hole is known as short-call, where you go to urinate. The other hole is usually deeper and is known as long-call, and you can guess what you do in this hole. We stand or squat over the appropriate hole in order to do our business.

A guest tukul was always on our compound because Baba had many visitors pass through to see him. Once we began to settle down in Nyau, Baba built a sleeping tukul first. I slept in his tukul, but I had my own mat. I guess I slept there until I was five or so. I don't really recall the move to independent sleeping quarters.

Our neighbors cleared and built their compound some distance away. Paths were cleared so we could reach each other and share life together, easily. I slept on a straw mat on the dirt floor, which I had to learn to put together. Our bed was made out of about twelve cut sticks of wood or branches, then elephant grasses are collected and laid on top of the lengths of wood, there is a kind of tree that you can strip to pieces to lie on as well.

A mosquito net is an essential item needed in South Sudan. Mosquitos are rampant and the majority of them are carrying malaria, so you want to protect yourself while you sleep. The net is hung above the bed and tucked in all around you so there are no breaches for the insects to enter.

One of the worst troubles I ever got in with Baba was about my mosquito net. Lets just say that I would punch holes in mine with my finger or maybe a little stick. I would throw it to the side getting up, or I would leave it lying on the ground and stomp all over it. Over time, the net was beginning to wear thin and fray and the more I pulled on it the bigger the holes became. Baba reminded me and warned me many times to take care of my net, but I didn't listen. The mosquitos started biting me more and more each night. So many of them were buzzing in my ears and the humming would drive me crazy. My hands were constantly swatting at the air while attempting to sleep, which was worse than the bite itself.

    I decided to complain to Baba. Oh goodness, that was the wrong idea. He made me use that holey net and refused to buy me another one. Holes or no holes in my net, Malaria is a major health problem in South Sudan. Ninety percent of all South Sudanese have had it, and I also contracted malaria many times in my life and it is a terrible kind of sickness.

    Male mosquitos feed on plants, but female mosquitos attack mainly at night because they need a blood meal in order for eggs to develop. A parasite from the female mosquito bite would get into my body and then came the aches, pains, chills, fever, nausea, and the headache, much like the flu. There was nothing to take to help with the symptoms; we had no aspirin, medicine, or doctors. I would simply lie on my straw mat until I felt strong enough to continue my daily routine. Thank you Lord for protecting me from the deadly forms of malaria and always being with me during my illnesses.

    When Baba would travel to share the word of God, he was usually gone three to four days but to me it seemed like forever. So, Deborah, Baba's oldest sister, who was married with no children and lived on the other side of the Yei River, would come to stay with me. It was a long way for her to walk, but she would come and go for many years as I was growing up. I remember walking with her holding my hand as we collected lulu nuts and leaves in the bush. Deborah would make porridge and take care of me like I was her own child. She cleaned the weeds from the garden once it was all planted and growing. Deborah had her own tukul waiting for her when she came to stay. Her husband passed away sometime during this journey and she came to live with us permanently. However, several years later she passed away as well, but I was old enough at this time to stay alone.

Termites are very aggressive in South Sudan and will eat and destroy a tukul within two years. Their mounds look like giant anthills that are sometimes more than 2ft tall. We often refer to them as flying white ants, but they really are not ants at all. Sudanese men spend most of their time rebuilding shelter for their family.

Fishing, cultivating, and hunting are other

activities that men perform frequently. They are hard working people that work from sun up to sun down with a little visiting along the way. Sharing meals together is part of our entertainment and we Sudanese love to talk, drink coffee, sip hot tea, and share stories. Our people are well known for their hospitality and we cherish and welcome guests. Yes, we could be Wal-Mart greeters with no training.

Baba is a person who never makes a fuss; he takes one day at a time and handles whatever comes up. But my ears can still hear him grumbling about termites eating our house and he is really grumpy when it does not rain. Our rainy season normally starts close to the end of March and it will rain hard and continuous April and May. In June, the drops slow down and then water from heaven is sporadic from July through October. Around early November it stops and the land dries up until end of March. When it starts to rain everyone is ready to begin cultivation of the garden. The earlier the rain begins to fall, the greater the results we have for a big harvest, and this is the prayer.

The Pride of Tribe

I was born into the African tribe who are considered farmers; therefore, we get going with planting corn, sesame, grains, peanuts, cassava, sorghum, and sweet potatoes. Morus depend on rain-fed crops to produce food. Remember those termites that ate our tukuls? Well, we eat them too along with roots fibers, leaves, and green vegetables throughout the rainy season. During the night a hole is dug in the ground a little distance from the termite mound and it serves as a pocket. Elephant grass is bunched or rolled together and lit on one end like a torch. This torch is held over the pocket hole. As the termites fly towards the light, the fire kills them and they drop into the pocket and are collected. To be honest termites are delicious but a little bit sandy. They are cooked and ground into a paste and then served as a delicacy. Termites have a nut-like taste and are very nutritious and have protein.

As a child, I recall being hungry and wanting food almost every single day. Hunger and malnutrition is a daily reality for children and adults in South Sudan. Even though we planted our garden, conditions didn't always make for a good harvest. Sometimes there was not enough rain and our crops were parched, and other times too much rain made for swampy crops, and often wild animals and insects sustained themselves on our food, and many times during the growing season we had to relocate quickly leaving our food behind. Once our harvest food was consumed, it was back to eating roots and leaves and searching the jungle for nourishment. Usually our one meal was right before bedtime so the hunger pangs would go away enough to get to sleep. To say I lived one meal at a time is totally true, but God provides all the nourishment needed for the life He had for me and also for the others each day.

Can you envision me playing outside in the dirt or working in the garden all day and then eating with my hands? That's exactly what happens because there are no eating utensils, no soap, or running water. Most of the food I ate was boiled or heated over the three-stone fire on the ground. I ate whatever was served with my fingers and it was not a big deal. I never knew any different, as this is life in South Sudan. I understand now that this causes worms and some of the illnesses we experienced in the jungle.

In order to clean my body or take a bath, about 8 cups of water are boiled over the three-stone fire. The water is put in a washbasin, carried behind a tree, and a cup is used to pour the water over my body. Roots were used for scrubbing the body oil, sweat, and dust off. I washed my clothes in a water bucket or a nearby dirty water source with roots as well. By the way, underclothes were not an available item in the jungle and I understand that this is called "going commando" in the States. I didn't get a haircut very often, but when I did, Baba used an old pair of scissors. Those scissors were not sharp so sometimes a shard of glass or a handsaw was used to trim my nappy hair. In the jungle it was a constant treasure hunt and we used whatever worked. This kind of living is nothing like anything you can fathom in the States.

During mango season (March), we were unable to walk about for the sweet, ripe mangoes were everywhere we looked. We happily were able to gorge ourselves on them. Each mango hangs from the tree like a giant, round Christmas tree decoration. When the fruits ripen, they fall and bounce on the ground as if the sky is falling. I can eat my weight in mangos but they are very expensive in the States so I have to limit myself. Have you ever eaten chocolate chip ice cream and mangos? I never thought in a million years this would be my bedtime snack, but it is delicious!

Visitors

In our house, Baba and I worked extra hard because we always had day-trippers coming and going in our compound. A lot of the time there were also strangers staying overnight. Pastors are well known in the area and everyone wanted to spend the night in his place when they were passing through to another village. Of course, these visits are not planned and can happen anytime of the day or night. This means there always has to be extra food and room for the travelers. Moru people do not raise their chickens (if we have one) for themselves. They save them for when visitors come. For me, I longed for visitors to come because I would be eating CHICKEN!! This was an exciting occasion, as my belly would be full and the pangs of hunger would cease temporarily.

Frequently, the guest would leave us with a token of appreciation. One token was a full-length heavy coat similar to what is known as a pea coat these days. I remember this coat very well. Baba graciously accepted it as we said goodbye to our visitor. As we prepared for bed, I clearly saw Baba taking his knife and cutting the coat in half, starting at the collar and down the back. I watched intently having no clue his mindset. He handed me one half and told me to use this as my blanket to stay warm. Most nights I was very scared in my tukul. I had fear of another attack or a large animal getting me.

This particular night as I crawled onto my bed, I used this coat to cover my whole body, including my head and toes. I did not leave an inch uncovered as I pulled my knees to my chest in a fetal position. This treasure allowed me to wrap myself up, so I could hide from anything and everything. Yes, I looked like a black cocoon in the elephant grass, but I slept like the most important king of all time. Every night, I could not wait to pull this coat, or by this time a blanket, over my head and rest.

Many years passed and as you can imagine this wool coat began to wear out. It was tattered and torn beyond repair, but I continued to wrap myself as best I could. One night as Baba was wishing me goodnight, he told me to wait until he returned before going to my tukul. Baba had safely kept and protected the other half of this coat just for me. Folded neatly and like brand new, Baba handed it to me. I was beyond excited and grateful for my sweet grandfather that God provided to take care of me. Even today, I continue to roll and conceal myself in a mound of covers, coats, or blankets regardless of the place or the temperature.

Hunting and Honey Harvesting

Collecting honey is another important duty of Moru men. We make traditional beehives, by taking some hay and tying it with a rope, before coating it with mud and putting it at the top of a tree for three to four months. Bees can also be found in caves building their own hives. Beekeeping is seasonal and honey is a very important food for Moru people.

Chapter Four - Moving On With Life

To harvest honey, we have to wait for the sun to set because in darkness all the bees are inside the hive or cave. Then, I climb the tree, set fire to the branch to smoke the bees, pray the bees don't attack me, reach into the hive to collect the honey with no gloves, and as a matter of fact, no protection at all. Honey is very sweet to eat but it is very hard to collect due to the difficulties associated with the process. It is a prized possession and if you visit a Moru family and they present to you some honey, this means you are considered a very important person to them. They are expressing their true friendship and how they value you as a person. In a marriage ceremony, honey is among the foods that will be eaten and sometimes the groom's family will present honey to the in-laws to show how much they love the bride. A long time ago it was used as part of the dowry price; what can be better than honey?

Many people have asked me, "How did Baba make money in South Sudan?" Well, we would dig our garden, pray, and hopefully harvest the crops, and sell, or barter any leftovers for what we needed at that time. We would trade corn, or cassava for coffee and tea. This was a constant process of juggling our resources to survive.

Hunting is not a sport in South Sudan; it is the real deal. We need meat, we need meat to eat! Many times the men hunted together as a community. Baba loved to hunt. It was his passion, like preaching, and if a morning hunt was scheduled, he would not sleep without anticipation. For my grandfather, hunting was like the Super Bowl or Alabama Football. Baba would wake up early to make me get my bow and arrows ready for the big day. This was the kind of day we longed for in our village. Baba's livelihood was energized and this motivated me to be like him. My grandfather was a very loud and outspoken man and he was known as the "screamer" in the village. Yes, he would stand in the middle of the woods and yell to the top of his lungs to scare the animals out of hiding. Baba's screams could be heard way in the distance, but he told me that his job was to encourage the hunters to kill something. As hunters, we killed any kind of animal or anything that crawled in the bush.

Miles and miles are trekked, killing bush rats, squirrels, or God-willing a bigger creature. The wildlife was carried home on our heads and smiles were bigger than ever. Everyone would be eating nourishment, regardless of his or her contribution. Wild animals in the jungle are just that - WILD! Let me tell you about a few of them that I have encountered.

Stray monkeys and baboons are all over the place and are really smart. The largest of several monkey species in South Sudan is the olive baboon. They will repeat your actions instantly. These baboons have giant teeth and roar really loud with their mouths open and heads back. One of these crazy creatures was attempting to invade our garden and was lurking in a nearby tree. I ran and retrieved my bow and arrow to get rid of him. I shot my arrow straight at the animal with no-heinie-hair and he caught it in mid air as it passed his body. I was stunned and stopped dead still in my tracks with my eyes not believing what I had seen. That baboon turned that arrow around and with his hands threw it like a spear back at me. He and I played this game for a while as I refused to give in to his shenanigans. He finally left and at least I got my arrows back.

Another day, I witnessed a lady with a broom trying to shoo away a baboon from her garden. She relentlessly was swinging and swatting at him to leave her compound. The lady returned to her tukul, leaving the broom propped beside the door outside. A few minutes later she exited her home and the baboon had that broom and began chasing her in the same manner. Many visitors have reported baboons harassing them by opening their mouths, showing their teeth, roaring, while holding and shaking their private parts. These crazy monkeys will make you laugh, but they are scary looking and they mean business.

Hyenas are another animal lurking in the jungle and require caution. They are on the prowl looking for food and I can hear them laughing in the distance when attempting to fall asleep. In some parts of South Sudan often children sleep in the trees to stay away from hunting hyenas. Thank goodness I never really encountered a close call with these fast, canine creatures like so many of my friends.

Chapter Five - Next Generation

Although missionaries had brought book learning and Christianity to the Moru tribe during the British colonial era, verbal history was still an important way for children to learn about their families, tribes, and traditions. Discussion of the skills of hunting, farming, collecting honey, building tukuls, and the Moru customs all took place around the evening fire, known as "Dumu tu dri," in Moru. As I sat and listened to the elders' experiences and war stories, and I learned so much. Baba would pull his chair near to the fire and praise me for my most recent accomplishments. Each night I gazed at the stars, watched the fire crackle, and listened to professor Baba teach me in the school of life. I had no idea that on the other side of the world there was television, video games, swing sets, phones, swimming pools, boats, or ice cream shops.

One recollection I have is a story about his English friend, who was a missionary in Mundri in the 1940s. Baba worked with him as a carpenter, and he loved that Baba was always on time. The missionary could not pronounce Baba's African name correctly so he nicknamed him, Jerry. The Englishman told Baba that he was a man of love, standards, quality, and performance. My grandfather was really impressed and excited that Jerry was his new name.

Baba wanted no grumbling, or complaining, and his rules were very straightforward. He expected me to obey and strive for excellence. Baba was a tough ole soul and did not play games. When I did not perform well or when I got out of line, Baba took action, though, of course, with love. He would send me to collect a switch for my spanking and I would return with the smallest twig that I thought would be approved. Usually, I would have to return to the woods for a larger, sturdier branch to be used on my bottom. I despised this pain and punishment.

When the fire burned down to red embers, we ended the day with evening prayers to our Father in Heaven. Like clockwork, this fireside chat took place seven (7) days per week, unless it was raining.

Education in South Sudan is a big deal. In order to survive, I had to learn how to live off of the land. South Sudanese girls grow-up learning by helping their mothers with their duties each day and they would discuss cultural responsibilities around the Katidri, which was another fire for cooking in Moru homes. Due to severe poverty, war, and lack of education, villages have no power, no roads, no running water, no stores, et cetera. Everybody in the family, no matter what the age, has a role to play in living life in South Sudan.

In the beginning, I had to sweep the area around the tukul and feed the chicken, that is, if we had one. As I got older, my tasks and duties increased based on my skill level. I learned from my grandfather at a very young age how to dig and plant a garden, about each seed type and how to fetch water from the nearest creek with a jerry can. Education has always been a priority in my life and my grandfather constantly encouraged me to learn and wanted for me to go to school more than anything. A school was set up in the place where the church would meet on Sunday. I would watch the older children leave for school and I could not wait until it was my turn to go.

Nowadays, there are Moru people who have lived outside the Moru tribe or outside of Sudan for a number of years. Their children do not have any knowledge about Moru traditional practices and Moru family education. It is now difficult for them to fit into the Moru community because they have not familiarized themselves with Moru practices. So it is absolutely important to be familiar with traditional practices. It is necessary for parents to give their sons and daughters both types of education: formal education through schooling and informal education or family education because both of them help to build a good society.

When I was eight (8) years old, my grandfather decided I was old enough to walk to school alone and learn from a man named, Henry Michael. Teacher Henry, as we called him, had completed a second grade education (from where I have no idea). He taught all the children who were just starting school from 1st grade to 7th grade, each group gathering under a different tree in the area. I would wake up with the sun and rinse off my face with dirty water. I brushed my teeth with a chew stick, which is a twig with a frayed end used to brush against the teeth. In Africa, chew sticks are made from a certain type of tree, also known as the "toothbrush tree". No breakfast before I began my long walk, arriving at school between 9:00-10:00am. I walked about three miles one way to get to the school tree and three miles home.

Under the School Tree

As soon as we arrived at the tree, all the students would have to clean the area by sweeping with elephant grass and set up our seating. We put rocks or tree trunks in rows but left enough space in front of them for writing in the dirt. Each of us found small sticks, which we used for writing the alphabet and counting. The master on duty would beat the drum around 11:00, and this was our sign it was time for class to begin.

Teacher Henry would speak in Moru, our tribal language, but we had to learn in English. I learned the alphabet, numbers, shapes and many other general British-English words. Teacher Henry would teach us a lesson, give us an assignment, and make us practice in the dirt with a stick, while he moved to the next class under another tree to teach. I loved going to school and was really sad if it was a rainy day because school would be cancelled. Most of the learning is based on memorization because the only thing you have is your brain. When it came to

Chapter Five - Next Generation

test time, I had to show the teacher in the dirt what I had learned. Teacher Henry always showed up and he was a nice man and a patient teacher. School was Monday through Thursday until around 3:00pm. No lunch, snack, or water was served during our school day. The walk home was slow with detours off the path into the woods looking for fruit or anything edible for now and later. Here is where I learned to write my name, and of course Teacher Henry taught us by Moru custom.

Male children are given five names. A Christian name (Bullen) and a Sudanese name (Dolli) are selected by your family at the naming ceremony. Next is your family name (Timo), followed by your father's name (Bennett), then your grandfather's name (Jangara). Due to my father's capture in the raid and my grandfather taking on the role of my dad/caregiver, my name is Bullen Dolli Timo Jangara Twili. I know in my heart God had all this planned and my name is perfect. Teacher Henry did not get paid for instructing these classes, but every Friday all students and their families had to go and dig the teacher's garden or clean his house, to show our appreciation. This was on a rotating schedule because we also had a garden to be worked at the school. At the end of the school year there would be a big festival using the food grown in the school garden and each student would receive their grade and promotion status in an announcement to the crowd.

Mean Kids

Festival was a giant celebration and I worked very hard to learn my lessons so I could move on to the next level of education under another tree. I was a scrawny boy with no parents, brothers, or sisters. Let me just say, "This only child obeyed all the rules." I had no one to fuss and fight with in my house ... there was no arguing with grandfather. I had no older sibling example to follow. I had no younger sibling to boss. I had no one to help defend me from the mean boys. Yes, we have bullies in South Sudan.

On my walk to school there was high wet elephant grass covered in morning dew. The blades were taller than me and I would have to pass through them. Carefully stepping and parting handfuls to the right and left, I would make my way. Several larger boys would rush from behind and push me down. My only clothes, just short of rags, would be all wet and messed up before I got to the school tree. I was so afraid of them and had no means of defense. My silly conclusion on why they would treat me like this was they wanted me to soak up all the dew to keep them dry while they go through. With miles to walk, this big shove wasn't likely to keep them dry. I was so nervous about my trek to school each day. I would delay as long as possible so the boys would be way ahead of me. My grandfather was on my nose to get going. "Boy, you must get to school." The bullies warned me if I reported what they were doing to my grandfather that would be the end of me. God helped me to press on

Chapter Five - Next Generation

and be thankful for the opportunity to go to school. God also used this to shape me into a compassionate young man caring for the "least of these". Although I was so scared, my goal was to go to school to learn lessons that would last me a lifetime.

One evening Baba returned home fairly early in the afternoon, so we began our normal routine early as well. At this time Baba had acquired a new tukul that was bigger than usual. It was large enough for him to have a small fire inside. I always had everything ready for Baba when he arrived home. The floors were swept, his bed was ready with a straightened net, the fire was lit, and water was boiled for coffee. We had our meal late afternoon and started the evening fire. I decided I was going to be sneaky; yes, this was premeditated as I was getting Baba's tukul tidied. I was weary of the mosquitos biting me and buzzing in my ears. I wanted a good night's sleep on Baba's comfortable bed with the warm fire to keep the bugs away. After chatting briefly with Baba, I went to his tukul, climbed in his bed, covered my head and lay really still. Maybe a half hour later, I hear him enter the room. I didn't move and pretended to be sound asleep. He mumbled, "What is going on here?" but he never touched me to wake me. I heard him lie down on the floor mat and we drifted off to sleep. Baba wakes up very early and was already sipping his coffee before I showed myself. As I sat down to say good morning, he looked across at me with his finger pointed toward my face and said, "YOU, if you think you are going back to sleep where you slept last night, that will be a joke". I think we were both chuckling inside as I just starred at him blank-faced without saying one word.

Saved

I did not hear the gospel in a church building or at a youth camp. I heard it around the fire from my grandfather. Baba was a strong man, who loved and cared for me. He understood the love of Christ and he shared it with me often. At the age of 13, I knew that I had no hope and that Christ was the only way I could continue to live. The Father drew me to Himself and I asked Christ to be Lord of my life. My life has never been the same. My grandfather modeled for me how to walk with the Lord and taught me about the Bible. My past will always be my past, but I knew that by following Christ my future would be bright!

"For I consider that the sufferings of this present time are not worthy to be compared with the glory which shall be revealed in us. For the earnest expectation of the creation eagerly waits for the revealing of the sons of God. For the creation was subjected to futility, not willingly, but because of Him who subjected it in hope; because the creation itself also will be delivered from the bondage of corruption into the glorious liberty of the children of God. For we know that the whole creation groans and labors with birth pangs together until now. Not only that, but we also who have the first fruits of the Spirit, even we ourselves groan within ourselves, eagerly waiting for the adoption, the redemption of our body."

Romans 8:18-23

Chapter Six - Displaced Camp

In 1998, Baba thought the time had come for me to go and live with my distant relatives in Kotobi. I had finished my elementary school last year and was in a waiting period because of no schools in South Sudan. School under the tree was a little better there and my second cousin, Andrew, was close to my age. My grandfather was prepared for me to get the best education possible, regardless of the sacrifice. I traveled to Kotobi where Andrew and I began this journey of education together.

On the weekends, I would walk back to Mundri to see Baba and help him with the things that needed to be done for him. I would wake up early and walk back to Kotobi before school started on Monday. My feet and legs have walked thousands and thousands of miles so far in my life and the Lord has been with me every step of the way.

"Have I not commanded you?
Be strong and courageous!
Do not tremble or be dismayed,
for the Lord your God is
with you wherever you go."

Joshua 1:9

Our garden had a supply of cassava during this season and I needed some shoes and clothes to wear to school. So at the local market, I sold some cassava and went on a search for a pair of shoes. I found a pair that had been brown at one time but due to age and wear had almost no color at all. The soles were still in place, so I decided to purchase some shoe wax and polish them. I bought a small can of Kiwi, some plaid pants that looked like pajamas, and a white blousy jacket and made my way back home. I brushed the dust off my new shoes, opened my Kiwi and with the little brush inside and I began to paint. After every square inch of this shoe was covered, I was so excited that I have these red shoes for walking. Yep, my shoes were RED as can be and I looked at the Kiwi can and the color says cordovan, but I have no idea what this means. I have never heard of this color in my life.

Taking Refuge in a Foxhole

Let me tell you about foxholes. It is a hole dug in the ground about 3 feet deep and is used for protection from aerial bombardment. A foxhole is the safe place where we spent much time when the enemy came to destroy our village. The bigger your family, the bigger the foxhole has to be to accommodate everyone, including any visitors. The noise of

Chapter Six - Displaced Camp

incoming disaster can happen anytime of the day or night, but Sundays, when Christians come together for worship, the government of Sudan will always schedule to send the aircraft. They know many worshipers will be in one place and one drop will wipe out many humans.

Helicopter gunships came and destroyed whole villages in late 90s. In Kotobi, the displaced camp is where many people lost their lives and churches were burned to the ground. Tree schools also have foxholes where all the children can hide at the sound of war.

One day as Andrew and I were coming back home from school we were discussing what we had learned during the day. We were excitedly talking and scuffing through the dirt, wondering what more we will learn tomorrow. Suddenly, we hear a weird noise, but it is dry season and the wind is blowing very hard and your ear cannot pick up what noise you are hearing. Well, we continued walking and there in our sight is a war jet. Within seconds it is on top of us and people are running, screaming, and shouting to hide in the nearest foxhole. I can't just lie on the ground because when the bombs explode particles fly in every direction and slash everything in their path. For any chance of survival, I have to be below the ground in a hole and sometimes that is not enough. If the bomb makes a direct hit on your foxhole, then it is your time to meet your Creator.

I do not remember separating from Andrew, only scrambling to find a foxhole, which was not showing itself. With no time to spare, an overfull hole becomes visible and I jump in landing on top of a lady holding a tiny one-day-old baby. The mother had run and tossed the baby in the hole and left as if she had another rescue to accomplish. So many things are happening at one time it's hard to describe this scene.

As I looked around, I recognized two older ladies from church in the hole. I quickly instructed them to hold this baby tight and that I was going to cover myself over this little body. All we could do was stay down and pray that God would protect us. The warplane passed over us and the sky was silent for quite some time. We all knew the plane would circle back to our location. We quietly waited, and waited ... listening hard, thinking maybe it's gone, and then in the distance our ears catch wind of a rumble, and we knew, here comes the plane back to our location.

The baby was crying so hard and my heart hurt because this precious life had no idea what was happening. Seconds later a LOUD jet engine came low and close, releasing multiple bombs, which created an even louder explosion. Dust and smoke covered the air above and the ground shook, as my heart pounded. This particular missile attack lasted more than 45 minutes, passing back and forth in the blue sky above us. After what felt like forever, the warplane vanished and didn't return.

Kotobi was smoldering as we begin to climb out of the foxhole. As I pushed to my knees, I felt a burning sensation on my hand and looked down to see a stream of blood making its way from a wound. At this point the extent of my injury was unknown, but I shared my discovery with the ladies as I helped

Chapter Six - Displaced Camp

them to their feet. My left hand was hit by a bomb particle shooting through the chaos. I used part of my shirt to wrap my hand and stop the bleeding. Upon further inspection, it was a deep cut, but nothing life-threatening. The rest of the day was spent inspecting the damage. The landscape was destroyed, metal shards everywhere, I looked and huge craters were now a part of Kotobi.

Everyone to some degree was shaken, but we Sudanese can still tell and retell our experiences with one another. Many people were injured and others lost their lives. The mother and the one-day-old baby were reunited and happy to be safe. Bearing the scar of war on my left hand, God protected all of us in this particular foxhole. Growing up in a war torn environment has impacted my life in so many different ways that I could never put it all into words. We were all thankful to be alive and life will go on and this will happen again. Oh how my life will be forever affected by this war. Every time I hear a loud bang or unexpected kaboom, my mind immediately reels back to being gunned down and my body shakes expecting something terrible to happen. I want to run to a safe place, but the only place I can find is into Jesus' arms.

"The name of the Lord is a strong tower;
The righteous run to it and are safe."

Proverbs 18:10

Chapter Seven - Missionary Impact

As time marched on, missionaries from South Africa came to encourage our people during the most difficult time in our history. It is difficult for foreigners to enter our country due to the ongoing warfare. South Sudan was cut off from the outside world and other countries have had no notion of what has been transpiring in South Sudan during these years.

Dr. Peter Hammond, the director of Frontline Fellowship, came to Moruland to share the gospel and teach the Great Commission to those who were under fire. He had a great heart for us in South Sudan and was determined to help. After consulting with the church leaders, Dr. Hammond started the first Christian high school in Mundri in April 2000. My grandfather attended the conference and returned home telling of the blessings the pastors had received. He was loaded down with books including the Old and New Testament in Moru. This was the first Moru Bible. Baba could not stop talking about all that he had learned and told me the announcement about Dr. Hammond opening a school.

Baba explained how much he wanted me to attend this school, but only a few students would be able to attend in the first year. I was excited Baba had been to the conference to hear this information. Dr. Hammond told the pastors how the interview process would take place, with an interview and a written essay being required. The essay needed to describe how I became a Christ Follower and why I wanted to attend school. My thinking cap was composing and I began to write in the dirt my answers. Baba clarified, "This is not what I heard. I think you are going to write using pen and paper." With eyebrows raised and eyes wide open, I looked at him with serious doubt. Where am I going to get this pen and paper?

The team repaired an old brick building with missile holes, which had been damaged by the war, for the new school and dorm. An announcement was made through the churches about an interview process that would take place to enter this school named Christian Liberty High School. Boy, did this word spread quickly through the villages. Andrew and I prayed together before departing for the church to have an interview. As we approached the church, there were mega people waiting, over 800 standing in line. I didn't really know what the first year number was going to be, but I knew it was few. Andrew and I glanced at each other thinking, "Oh my goodness, how is this ever going to happen?"

At the age of 16, I applied and was granted an interview with Pastor Nelson. He was appointed to meet with each applicant and get to know his or her intentions. I was so nervous; I had no sense of how an interview would be done.

As I entered the room, Pastor Nelson greeted

me and then we took a seat across from each other. He began the conversation with small talk and then two questions: How did you become a Christian? And why do you want to go to school? I told Pastor Nelson about becoming a Christian at 13, and that I wanted to follow Christ. I explained that my purpose of going to school was to help my people. The Moru people need more wisdom and knowledge in order to be able to provide for themselves. I was so glad when this interview was over, but now I am anxious to hear the names of those picked for school.

It took a few days for Pastor Nelson to get finished with all of the interviews. Wesley Malish, the librarian-to-be at the new school, ran into us on the way home and after exchanging small talk, he secretly confessed that my name was among those who passed the interview. Is this for real? I will be going to a Christian High School! This was the best news I had heard in a long time. Praise God, I was chosen! I was one of fifty students going to school out of all those in line. For the first time in my life, I was able to use a pencil, paper, and a book. Although I had to break my pencil in half to share with others, I was still so excited. I received a uniform to wear and I learned to march in lines and sing songs with friends. I lived in a large room with bunk beds and my classes included Bible, history, arithmetic, and English, and all at NO COST! God used his servant people and brought them to teach us and He covered the payment.

    This school was unlike the tree school, with a ton to learn and so many new friends from South Africa. Most of the teachers were on short-term mission and would come and go over a period of time. Did I tell you I love to meet new people? I met two Americans, Beth G and Timothy Keller, with whom I became really close friends, and this encounter impacted my life tremendously. Beth was a nurse and also my teacher at school. She taught Math and Bible. Our first Bible study was on the book of Hebrews and was like nothing I had ever done before. Beth also taught small children in the mornings to memorize scripture. Loice, one of my fellow students, helped Beth with the children, and I helped in translating. Timothy and I became close and our friendship grew strong. He and I traveled to villages to share the gospel and show the love of Christ. Many individuals came to accept the Lord as their Savior.

    I will never forget their names or faces nor how much Beth and Timothy influenced my life. God continues to provide and allow me the beginning of an education that I could not afford. However, this historical school opening didn't last long. After six short months, it draws the attention of radical Muslims that South Sudanese children were learning in a school and they bombed our school many times by aircraft. As a result, the missionaries left and the school was closed. My heart was broken because I wanted to learn more, but I trusted that God had a plan. I had a taste of what real school would be like and I wanted it desperately. Once again my high hopes of getting an education were fading and I had no idea what would be next. Baba and I continued to pray and trust that the Lord would make a way even when there seemed to be no way.

> *"Blessed is the man who trusts in the Lord, and whose hope is the Lord. For he shall be like a tree planted by the waters, Which spreads out its roots by the river, And will not fear when heat comes; But its leaf will be green, And will not be anxious in the year of drought, Nor will cease from yielding fruit"*
>
> **Jeremiah 17:7-8**

Living off the land has all its joys and difficulties. South Sudan has one of the deadliest snakes in the world. One morning I went to the garden to get a pumpkin to prepare a meal. As my eyes searched for a ripe pumpkin, a black mamba hiding under the leaves struck me twice on the leg, and so blind and paralyzed within minutes, a neighbor in her garden heard my screams ... my leg began to swell. Friends picked me up and carried me to my tukul, and I could hear them talking to me, but I could not respond. There was more swelling until my brown skin burst with poison ... terrible pain you cannot believe. I was unable to see the fluid running from my eyes and nose, and I thought my time had come to see Jesus.

My favorite teacher, American nurse, Beth, was in Mundri at the time and my friends told her about the snakebite. She rushed to give me some anti-venom, but my friends and those taking care of me refused. They were afraid the shot of medicine would kill me. In the jungle we didn't understand about medicine and that it would have helped my little body. My friends and neighbors continually prayed over me and stayed by my side for weeks. God healed me! This life is a walk of faith I will never forget, and I will use my experiences to glorify God by bringing hope to the people of South Sudan.

This was not my only encounter with a snake. Mambas like to chase you! Timothy Keller, a great friend and I went to a village about 38 miles South of Mundri to share the gospel and show the Jesus film. On our way back we come head to head with this fearless snake. We were riding my bicycle and as I glanced around I see a snake squirming quickly towards us. Do you know how fast these skinny legs can pedal? Really really fast! To this day, I do NOT like to see a snake on TV or in person; it reminds me of the hardship I faced on a daily basis and makes my stomach hurt.

I love Beth so much and always wanted to give her a token of my appreciation. I can still remember this one-day my grandmother, Penina, gave me a chicken to take home with me. I took that chicken right to my friend Beth. I showed up at her tukul and told her I wanted her to have this chicken.

She was mortified. She knew how hungry and malnourished I was, but she didn't want to hurt my feelings. Of course, I didn't understand this at the time, and she told me to take that chicken home but I begged her from my heart to take it and she did.

As I longed and hoped for more missionaries to come to Mundri, I would run to meet whoever came to our village. I was a talker and I can remember names of people very well. I was so excited to learn anything they would share with me and I love to meet new people. I worked each day around the local church doing anything asked of me.

After two years of trusting God to complete the work that He started in me, my cry was heard. My friend, Timothy Keller, an American missionary, came back from South Africa with other missionaries. They came to Kotobi and Timothy was asking everyone about my whereabouts. All of the students were scattered because school was closed. I received notice from a friend that Timothy was looking for me in the village. I came quickly and was so happy to see him again. He told me to get ready so that we can go to Lui for discipleship training. After several days with those Americans they questioned, "Why are you here at this church? You should be in school." I explained there was no school here and in order to continue any education I would have to travel to another country. This team of missionaries wanted to help me go to school and promised to return to the States and see what they could work out. Timothy introduced me to Billy, Jesse, Daniel, and so many others on the team.

We crowded into an old Toyota truck and hit the road to Lui. After approximately 15 miles, the truck quit, and we walked the remainder of the way. It was actually nice to walk rather than driving 5 miles per hour on the pothole filled roads that had been destroyed long ago. It was late in the night when we finally arrived, and it was time to sleep.

At sunup I was ready for coffee, hot tea, and the conference. What a joy to be with fellow believers and share God's word with one another. The weeklong meeting was wonderful and I hated to say good-bye to my friends again. God was weaving His plan together without our knowledge. Billy, the team leader for ITAM (It Took A Miracle) Ministry from Knoxville, Tennessee, and I, prayed, thanking the Lord for our friendship and our time together. Jesse and Daniel prayed over Andrew and I as well. Our prayers for each other were heartfelt and all of us knew we would never forget one another. We promised to meet again but we didn't know if it would be on earth or in heaven. In this place where I reside, we live for today and do not plan for tomorrow because it may not be yours.

In 2003, through the help of missionaries, God opened the door and granted me opportunity to travel to a neighboring country, Uganda, where I would be able to continue my education. My grandfather and I were excited about this good news. I traveled to Kampala and enrolled in Cityside College Makerere to attend my high school. The high school years are called college or secondary school in Africa. The travel to school took a couple of days on multiple buses and crossing the border to another country. This ride was costly and each time I crossed the border there was a fee to be paid as well. I couldn't just return to Mundri to visit Baba and communication was slim. This adventure to Uganda was not without many trials, but God has been so faithful in providing my every need. God has used many people to show His glory and He has taught me to walk by faith, not by sight.

The following year, ITAM returned to Mundri with another group of missionaries from America to share the love of Christ and preach the gospel. On this team was the co-founder of Four Corners Ministries, Jimmy Sprayberry, who had heard about Mundri, South Sudan, and our situation from all the publicity through the Southern Baptist convention. Jimmy went to help children on a mission trip to Venezuela and met Billy and ITAM missionaries there. ITAM invited him to join them in coming to

South Sudan. David Platt, a young man who had a passion to share Christ with the Nations, was among the team. Since I was already in Uganda going to school, you are not going to believe what happened. I received a phone call from Mission Aviation Fellowship (MAF) in the main office at school. These guys called to let me know that I had been booked to fly to South Sudan. I do not know about your first flight experience but for me this was big news. "This boy is about to fly!" This was the best fun ever and I sure did enjoy this fast travel to Mundri. Looking down on the land was amazing and I could see God's creation for miles and miles.

> *"This is what the Lord says the Holy One of Israel and your Creator: "Do you question what I do for my children? Do you give me orders about the work of my hands? I am the one who made the earth and created people to live on it. With my hands I stretched out the heavens. All the stars are at my command. I will raise up Cyrus to fulfill my righteous purpose, and I will guide his actions. He will restore my city and free my captive people, without seeking a reward. I, the Lord of Heaven, Armies, have spoken!""*
>
> **Isaiah 45:11-13**

Chapter Eight - The Search Is On

Then in 2005, a peace treaty was signed in Sudan to end the war between the North and the South. The time had come to emerge from our war torn area and begin looking for friends and relatives. I considered myself one blessed young man. I will never take for granted my grandfather and many other people who raised me during the time of war. Baba used his gifts and talents very well and I am grateful that I had this golden opportunity and privilege of sharing life with him. There is nothing to be regretful about in life if it does not go the way you thought. God's mercies are new every morning and His faithfulness has reached the sky. Enjoy every single moment of life that God has given to you. It is a great gift! In life the most important thing is to know and trust in the Giver of Life. I am not saying it was easy, but at least we know that we are in HIS plan.

Word was spreading that families could possibly be reunited in the capital city of Juba. I really wanted to see my immediate family again. Andrew and I began figuring a plan on how to travel to Juba by asking for suggestions from fellow Moru. We did not own a bicycle but a cousin of Andrew, named Paul and his friend Jackson, volunteered to carry us on their bicycles. With only two bicycles, the four of us set out peddling our way from Kotobi to Juba, taking turns steering. This ride is about 127 miles on decade old dirt roads with potholes bigger than the bike. I had no way to know how long this would take. We cycled all day long and spent the first night at a military base on the way. Road signs were few along the washed out roads. Trees were growing over the roads and bushes were taking over the sides of the paths. War has taken its toll on not only humans, but also the infrastructure. This landscape was a horrible site.

While preparing to depart from base, the army officer explained about land mines we were about to encounter in the next four miles. Landmines have been connected and networked in this area for over twenty years. We inquired of another route, but this was the only passage to Juba. The four of us sit down to discuss the risks involved in continuing our quest. The army officer was very clear, many people have traveled through but only a few made it safely. The process would be very slow and each step must be calculated and looked at closely. This kind of news was not something I was anticipating to hear.

I have seen with my eyes the injuries and deaths due to landmines. One wrong move and it's over. I contemplated quickly the past and I knew the seriousness of our situation, but I also wanted to see if my family was alive no matter the cost. All four of us had to trod over miles of land with two bicycles and not touch a landmine. This was not going to be fun. We prayed and knowing God is in control, we agreed to press on across this land. Our bodies shaking and moving like a turtle to avoid a wrong move, we saw thousands of landmines. I mean THOUSANDS! We were quiet and creeping, trying to communicate and figure our every step. I wonder why we were whispering because there was no one else around and the landmines can't hear. I do not know how to explain how anxious I was or my feelings as we made our way through this area. After long hours of stepping on grass roots, a few scratches, and sweat dripping from our bodies, we were standing on the other side in the Sudan government controlled area.

A military guard met us as we exited the tall grass field. We were immediately interrogated as to who we were. We explained to him we were civilians on our way to Juba. I told him I was separated from my entire family when I was about four (4) and that I was on my way to look for them. He told us to continue on our journey. We couldn't believe the road; it was still dirt but not washed out. As we continued there were multiple stops by armed guards on the way and the same question was asked again and again. Finally, we arrived in Juba, the capital of South Sudan. There was a big gate standing before me and the unknown status of my family's existence was overwhelming. I had to check in at the main entrance by standing in line that was a mile long wait.

Once at the processing center, I had to give my name, my father's name, grandfather's name, great grandfather's name, and any other information I might know on both sides of my family. They wanted to know my tribe and from where was I coming. This process took forever and I do not know how many hours I had to stand in the blazing heat.

Finding Mother

As the registration was in progress and I was telling as much information as I could recall, I had no idea there was a Moru man from our tribe listening nearby. I finished and glanced in front of me at an enormous tent city with people on every inch and in every direction. My ears could hear multiple languages all around me. This gentleman approached me and greeted me speaking my Moru language.

This was the first sign from the Lord that I was going to be okay. I introduced myself and inquired about whether he knew any other people here from the Mundri area. I needed to find a preacher, a community leader, a friend of the family, or anyone that might have information on my mom, dad, brothers, or sister. He was very nice and friendly, but was unfamiliar with the Timo family. He did know some other people who might be helpful in my search. I am beginning to see how finding "the missing or dead" requires the whole world. There was a Mundri community leader living in Juba and he knew where to find Andrew's sister's house. Vida is a cousin to my dad and she knew where my family was staying. Oh how amazing is this? I could feel the hugs and warmth of my mom and dad and I was not even there yet.

While being escorted on our bicycles for two hours to their last location, my mind imagined what my mom now looked like, and how big my brothers might be and whether they would recognize me, and what would my dad say...what was I going to see?

This had been on my mind the whole way, but then it was really swirling in my brain. Exhausted, hot, hungry, and thirsty, we rolled up to Vida's. She immediately gave us food and water and we rested. My mind was still reeling, but I was trying to be sociable and excited to see Andrew's cousin.

Our Mundri guide finally left and it was time to head to my family's place. It is very true that Sudanese don't get in a hurry, but this day I was in a hurry. At the first step, my heart was pounding very fast. It was not too far of a walk and I saw a little lady sitting outside of her small tukul. I was looking at her very hard, hoping I could call up in my mind what she looked like. I just knew that was my mom. I yelled loudly, "Mama is that you?" and she sat really still wondering what was happening.

She responded, "Dolli, Tata, my son is this you? Oh God, thank you, thank you God, You did not forget me. I thought I was forgotten, but You do not forget me. Thank you Jesus, thank you Lord!" I ran to her. We jumped for joy and held each other crying and crying and crying and could not believe this was happening. I thought it was a dream because I had been dreaming many times for many years. This day was not a dream, it was not a dream anymore, and this was a reality! We could not let go of each other and I was thinking, "Where is the rest of us?"

Within a few minutes, I noticed that it was just mom and my sister, Kamala, and I. We were still shedding tears of joy and Mary told me my father and all of my five brothers passed away. She said, "I thought you had died too, but I am thankful that you are alive and here with your sister and me."

My search began in Juba and thankfully my search ended there as well. By God's grace, I found my mother and my sister, but I was saddened to hear that all five of my brothers were killed and my father had died as well.

Yet my mother's heart was filled with joy of seeing that I was alive and well, and I knew that our reunion was just another part of the greatness of God in my life. I have to be honest in saying I was still devastated with this news. This reunion was bitter- sweet for me. My mom continued, "You have a half-brother whose name is Paul. During the war, the army recruited your dad. We were separated for over nine years, with absolutely no communication between us. Dolli, we assumed each other's death had taken place and your dad remarried a lady by the name of Nadi. Together they had a child, Paul. Ten years later, your dad was sent back to Juba and there he found me alive! Shocked and stunned, your father told Nadi goodbye and reunited with me." My mother clarified her understanding and loved my father dearly.

Remember the Moru culture when I had to go

with my grandfather in Nyau? When a baby is born, it has to be raised by the father or the family of the father. Therefore, Paul joined our family to be raised by Bennett and Mary. When my dad passed away from a health crisis, my mom is still responsible for Paul, and she took care of him. God has given us a blessing in Paul as a member of our clan and as the oldest living male, I am now responsible for my family. Kamala, mom, and I had so much catching up that the words couldn't come out fast enough. Each day together more and more information was shared as we told of our past fifteen years.

My Father

My mom shared great details with me about my father. I longed to hear more and more stories, trying to remember and cherish this man I had hoped to find. My mom said, "Your father hunted hard to feed all of you children. He loved his family with his whole heart and wanted to raise his boys to do the same. He strived to be an example for others to see. Bennett was well known in Mundri for making nice African dresses for both men and women. He was an excellent tailor and word spread about his talent. Before Christmas and holidays, many people wanted new clothes made by him. His love for soccer was deep. He traveled to play in other parts of South Sudan and later became a referee in the community before he joined the army. Bennett was active in the village and had few to talk about and he would never speak negative about others."
Mother began telling me this story that made my

heart sing and smile inside. "Every time when my father came back home from working, I would come sneaking up behind him, jump on his back and hug his neck and he would say, "Who is this one holding my neck?"and I would respond to him with a small voice, "This is somebody." If my dad came in and I didn't come running, he would ask, "Where is somebody? Can he come to see me?" Oh what a memory, what a time, oh what a short time of a father son friendship and relationship.

New Beginning

Each new morning we woke up as family, thanking and rejoicing for what God had, has, and will do for us. I just had so many questions to ask mom.
"What was life like before all the chaos broke out when I was barely four (4) years old?"
My sweet mom began to tell me all about our life before the war. I could see and hear in her voice that she was struggling as she relived the story. Tears streamed and her voice cracked while she was telling all the old memories. Mom said, "There is nothing we can change about what has happened in the past, but we can follow God as He is leading us into the future. Let's thank God that all three of us are alive and that we can make it." This was so encouraging for me, and I knew at this moment that my mom was a tough and strong woman. She continued, "It is not an easy road we are walking but God walks beside us and He will lead us through this journey too."
I shared that I have seen God's hand and He had

walked with me in these fifteen years. I have assurance that He would not let us down and never fail us. I recounted to her the story of my salvation and how my grandfather shared the gospel with me. I proclaimed how God changed my heart! She was overjoyed and we all rejoiced together.

Mom and Samuel, my nephew

Today my sister is married to Ruben and God has blessed them with three wonderful children, Samuel, Sura, and Ester. We have been through a lot in life but we have a bright time ahead. Life is a passage on this earth and we have to take it as it unfolds. There is an old saying, "You cannot control the wind, but you can control your boat." Bullen says, "I cannot control my boat. Christ controls it and He is the Captain of my life. It is the only way to make it." For me to be reunited with my mother and sister is a great victory that I will celebrate for the rest of my existence.

My mom described to me her time in captivity. Mary was kept in Juba for countless years and was not allowed out of a certain area of the city. Nobody could enter the town either. This was like a prison with one meal a day. Some days there were no rations at all. Mother witnessed many deaths from hunger and starvation. With no medicine, disease was rampant and deadly as well. Many believers in Christ suffered at the hands of the extreme radical Muslims. Mary is very active and fast in everything. She does not want to wait. She was born ready and cannot waste any time. She loves to share with her friends and if anyone comes to her house and are in need of anything, what she has she will give. Kamala and I call her "Girani" which means "neighbor" because mom's motto is always "Love your neighbor as yourself."

Growing up with only my grandfather, numerous times I would think of my mom and how I would love to play with my siblings. I just kept thinking that one day this was going to happen. Growing up I did everything by myself. I am that kid who can do it or figure it out for himself. It might not be correct, but it will be done. This position makes me strong. When I had trouble or discouragement, I encouraged myself and pulled myself up. Many days and stories later, my mom looked at me and said, "Bullen, I am so proud of you and you are so encouraging to me." I said, "Mom, you are a strong woman and you have encouraged me. You are in your 50s, you lost your husband and your children, you have a stepchild, and you are still standing strong. That is encouraging!"

My heart was exploding with love and appreciation to God, who had been so faithful and His grace so sufficient for me. It would have been really hard if I had not found my mom and sister in Juba, but God chose our reunion. Many thousands of people were not able to reunite with their brothers, sisters, or even their parents. The war in Sudan left many orphans, widows, and missing family members. This war redesigned my entire life and I will tell this God story to my children. War is never a good thing but has happened since the beginning of this sinful world. This war has ceased for now but the pain is still very genuine. A new nation was born but the suffering is still among us and we will never forget our heritage. War wounds will be healed but scars will remain with us for the rest of our lives.

Chapter Nine - USA Adventure

In 2006, ITAM invited me and three other Sudanese to come and share the stories of suffering of people in Sudan to the churches in the United States to raise money for our villages. Jeffrey, Stephen, Andrew, and myself were heading to Knoxville, Tennessee. We would be speaking in many different venues and areas throughout the States. For this reason, Andrew and I did not attend school during this time and we began the process of paperwork for a visa at the first of the year. It took a long time and we had to visit the US Embassy for multiple interviews. After four long months of waiting, our visas were granted for travel. Hallelujah!

While at Cityside High School, Uganda

However, the evening we were set to depart for the US, we were stopped and told to return to Kampala, Uganda. A document was missing. A visa to the Netherlands was required for travel; therefore, we lost our flights. All of us were so confused as to what was going on. A visa to the Netherlands? Here we are ready to fly and have to go back and get another visa? I had no clue how many US dollars this involved at the time, but I sure know now. Not one of us was willing to give up, finding the Netherlands Embassy was our mission. Once we arrived there, guess what, it was not open and a representative only works a few days a week.

Another waiting period and here we stood, four Sudanese looking for a needle in a haystack as we did not know what in the world we were doing. Finally, the Netherlands visa was granted and we were told it would get us from one gate to another at the airport. We were cutting up with each other in Moru, as this makes no sense. It was now time to head to the States.

Our expedition officially began from Kampala, Uganda, to the Netherlands, on an eight-hour flight that was amazing. I had experienced nothing like this before; the food, coffee, tea and much more are served many times. The flight guy came and asked what I wanted to eat and I told him, food. He said what kind of food and I repeated to him, I would appreciate it if you could give me food. I did not know how to respond and eventually this man figured out that I did not know the meaning of a menu. The flight attendant showed me there was a variety of food and which one would I like to eat? I was so confused at this time, I told him to just give me one. I could feel from his look he was getting fed up with me and ready to move on down the aisle. He handed me a food tray that was loaded and I was amazed at the amount of food on the plate in front of me.

Can I tell you, this was the first time I ever saw a little yellow square wrapped in paper? To the touch it was slippery. I did not know what to do with it. Of course, there was salad and I understood these are leaves to eat, but to me they needed to be cooked before I could eat them. Why are these on my plate? I casually looked around to see what the other passengers were doing with this yellow square, so I could apply it myself. Smart man, huh?

I figured out a long time ago if you do not understand what is before you, just take your time and watch what others are doing. Yes, it worked. This slippery thing goes on your bread and it is called butter. I saw people eating their leaves, so I joined them and ate too. Next the flight attendant gave me some ice. Yikes, it was cold! Was I supposed to eat this? I experienced so much in eight hours; what more was I going to encounter? My mind had never thought this hard before.

The plane landed in the Netherlands and boy this was another story. WOW! Moving steps were crazy for all of us, but learning to maneuver on them was an adventure. I was sure everyone who was sitting in the airport noticed that we were not familiar with this environment.

We got to next gate for our plane that would take us to Atlanta, Georgia. Another long flight, but I was experienced this time and we made it to the United States. Once we arrived, it took five long hours before the immigration officer told us, "Welcome to America." Each time my eyes looked around, something new appeared. This was not easy but all worked according to the will of God, and now we were officially in the United States of America.

I could not believe this dream was becoming a reality. The following morning we hit the road to Knoxville, Tennessee, and my cultural shock continued. How could all these things be so different on the other side of the world? Bathrooms were the most confusing; somebody had to teach me how to operate this big white bowl. I was thinking, "Why are we wasting all this clean water to go to the bathroom?" The shower. Oh, how I loved the shower!!! I enjoy how it "rains" on me and how excited I was to feel clean. I was staying with Jesse and his wife Kayla, who had come to visit me in Mundri. Jesse asked, "What have you enjoyed the most so far?" My response was, "The shower. It has to be the SHOWER!"

Going to a restaurant to eat was a great occasion. There were lists and lists of different food and drink. People served us and brought us whatever we needed. I wish I had a picture of my mind and face when we pulled up to a speaker in the drive-thru to order food to go. Now that was one of the most amazing things I have ever seen. Many dishes of food are served cold, like a ham sandwich, but I like my food hot, very hot. We had zebras running all around in my country and in the States, I am eating zebra cakes for dessert.

A dear friend, John and his wife, Kim, and their two children, took us to a place called Target to buy clothes and shoes. Needless to say, Jeffreys, Stephen, Andrew and I were fired up and speaking a foreign language to each other. As the doors opened automatically and we stepped inside, we could not believe all that our eyes saw. One funny fact of our discovery, "Who knew that clothes had sizes?" None of us knew how to answer clothes or shoe sizes. After many attempts of putting on different shoes, size seven (7) shoes worked for me and now it was time to try on pants and shirts. So many choices before me; what to wear, what to eat, what to drink, and all I know is that back home you eat once a day and you drink water if you are blessed. Here, each day we were served breakfast, lunch, and dinner. It was oh so good and my stomach has never felt like this before. After a few days, my mind drifted back to my people in Mundri who are starving and thirsty. They are drinking dirty water and hungry and dying from lack of food and nutrition. My mind battled every single day with these constant reminders of war and the people I had left behind. I praised God for picking me to be the recipient of these choices and this travel. It is bitter sweet as I observed and acquired skills like never before to be able to return and help my Moruland.

    On Good Friday evening, we decided to go for prayers at one of the largest churches in the area. We gathered in the churchyard forming a circle and holding hands as we began to sing one of my favorite hymns. We were belting out, "There is a fountain filled with blood," in Moru, and our American friends were singing in English, "Oh what a melody to our God." Then with heads bowed and eyes closed and praying, out of the blue some guy started his motorcycle and the noise was just like gunfire - and so in the middle of prayers I was screaming, "It is here!!!" My mind thought I was in Sudan and somebody had heard us singing and they were coming after us. The missionary, Billy, called to me, "Bullen, it is okay that is just a boda-boda (motorcycle)." I was like, "Motorcycle? Here in the deep jungle in the middle of night?" I forgot I was in America! During this adventure there were many times where I woke up from a dead sleep in the middle of the night with no recollection of where I was on this planet and this was not fun. I asked myself, "Am I dreaming?" Yes, I have lived through dozens of times like this in the bush. The next time was very different; I was in a hotel room in Atlanta, Ga.

My experiences were funny to me, and I was happy, enlightened, and it was unforgettable. The ninety or so days here in America, traveling from state to state was an experience I will never ever forget. My eyes saw the countless grains of sand on the beach and the vast ocean was not what my mind had thought. As far as my eye could see was water

Chapter Nine - USA Adventure

touching the sky with puffy white clouds everywhere. It was so beautiful and proclaimed the greatness of our God.

Beignets in New Orleans with the sweetest white powder and strong coffee was a special treat. The sight of many people using cell phones to communicate constantly was unbelievable. In every state, I searched and looked around for the money tree that was so talked about and discussed in my country. Guess what? I never found one because it doesn't exist. A U.S. dollar is not picked from a tree in the back yard; they are obtained by working hard.

I encountered different cultures, heard many different pastors preach the Word of God, and I myself spoke at different churches of multiple denominations, traveled to numerous cities and venues, ate food I didn't even know existed, met thousands of people, had back pain from a strain like I have never felt before, made new friends for life, talked on the radio and television, slept in places and on beds that my mind had never fathomed, viewed six (6) lane roads with cars moving in every direction, learned about computer communications at its finest, and most of all everything was just so CLEAN! God was allowing me to see how people live so differently yet so much the same thousands of miles around the world. God was showing Himself greater than all my fears.

The return flight back to Africa was just as adventurous as the travel to the States, but in a different sort of way. So many generous people had given to us in America items to take home. What we didn't understand was that there was a weight limit for each suitcase and we could only have two pieces of luggage each, and all of these were airline rules. All of us had crammed so many books, and so much clothing, shoes, souvenirs, et cetera, into our luggage that the scales tipped and the cost was too much. Items had to be rearranged and removed in quick fashion. Billy was tossing and weighing, shuffling, and removing things from our bags as we stood feeling victimized and wounded. We were all so excited about our new books and gifts from America.

    Baffled and sad, not understanding what had just taken place, we proceeded through the security line alone, making our way to the departure gate listed on our ticket. The luggage ordeal had taken too long and we missed our flight. Here the four of us stood in an airport over 4000 miles from home with no means of communication. Thank goodness we understood English enough to get from point A to point B. We had no experience in booking flights, no phone, no place to sleep, and our travel back home took us over 7 days. Yes, you read that correctly, we missed every single connection in every country. Each of us learned so much about international travel; something we didn't even know could be an issue on the red dirt roads of South Sudan.

    I will always be deeply thankful for all the golden opportunities that God has given to me. God chose me to go to other countries and share about my fellow brethren who are unable to speak for themselves. I enjoyed from my heart to be a voice for them and tell their stories to other people around the world. What I know from experience is that it is not easy to forget the stories we hear about other people.

But it will be even harder to forget the suffering of loved ones, especially when you have suffered with them. I tell you the truth, if you have been part of war or starvation and it has affected your life, then your life will never be the same again.

"If one member suffers, all suffer together; if one member is honored, all rejoice together"

1 Corinthians 12:26

Many times as Christ followers we tend to forget that we are all children of the King, regardless of our color, nationality, or ethnicity. We all belong to the kingdom of heaven and those who are suffering around the world, wherever they are, if they are Christ followers then we are one. If our brethren are being persecuted, we are with them because they are suffering for the same faith that we have and they are proclaiming the Lord Jesus Christ. I always say that I am a Christ-follower who lives in South Sudan; the reality is I am not a citizen of any country but of heaven and you can be too. You may be living in America or Europe or anywhere in the world but if you trust in Christ you are no longer a citizen of this world. Therefore, brothers and sisters, let us never neglect the suffering of our families around the world. We are one body and if one suffers, we all suffer.

Chapter Ten - More Studies

Upon our return to South Sudan, God provided for Andrew and I to continue our high school education in Uganda in 2007, through Four Corners Ministries. The school year started in January and I completed secondary school at the end of that year. Financial support from brothers and sisters in Christ in America sponsored my school tuition. As my communication and computer skills increased, I was able to go to the local Internet cafe and check my emails from new friends across the ocean. I never dreamed I could have this number of people to message.

I began having trouble seeing because my glasses were broken and expired. God went before me because I told no one about my eyesight. I received a message from someone in Alabama asking if I needed anything. I replied that I needed an eye exam and new glasses. The money was wired to me that very day and helped me to see clearly His provision. A funny story happened during this transaction of wiring money. When you send money to someone, a password is required to receive the funds. Well, the password given to me was "grape" by my American friend. I asked myself, "What in the world is "grape"?" I had no idea until I returned back to the land of the free and inquired to know the meaning of this word. I love grapes now!

Very few people in South Sudan will have the experience of attending college, but I knew in my heart that God had a different plan for me. In January 2008, Four Corners Ministries stepped out in faith to bring myself and Andrew to America to further our studies, so we could return to help our people in South Sudan. I was given the opportunity to apply for a student visa to travel to the United States. After eight long months of waiting and trusting, God saw fit for the Embassy to grant me my student visa. I could see my dream coming true. I was heading to the United States of America to attend college. Thank you, Lord!

Most people do not understand how blessed they are to live in freedom or even what that means or what that looks like. The copious amounts of paperwork and documents needed to bring one individual to the States to study are massive and a task beyond words. God is so good and I will be forever thankful for Tripp and his wife Sarah who completed all of this red tape and believed in helping me go to college. Tripp and Sarah, along with the community of Wadley, Alabama, welcomed me with open arms. Four Corners Ministries has been so much a part of my life. This ministry visited my homeland, walked with me during happy times, stood in the gap for me when I was in need of prayers and invested in my life as a human being who desperately wanted an education. The Educate Africa program has truly changed my life forever and I am so over-joyed that God allowed me to be a pioneer of this movement.

I began classes at Southern Union State Community College in Wadley, Alabama, in the Fall of 2008, arriving the day classes started. I hit the ground running and was amazed at how much could be done in a single day. My dorm was brand new and so many people helped me to get settled. I had a coffee pot, a small refrigerator, and a closet for my clothes, a nice bathroom, a shower, a really high off-the-ground bed and a syllabus for each class with so many instructions my head was spinning. I can tell you that math and keyboarding almost killed me. How in the world are you supposed to type on a keyboard without looking and go-fast with the letters and numbers in such random places? This was the craziest thing I had ever heard, and my fingers did not want me to pass this class.

There was a landline phone in my room, which made me jump every single time it rang. The cafeteria served three hot meals per day and I had all different kinds of food to eat. Learning the names of the types of food was another story. One food that was delicious was a hot dish of beans, tomatoes, and meat in a bowl. Every single night I received a call from my new mama who wanted to know what I had eaten, and I would describe it to her. She asked, "Chili?" I said, "No, it was not cold." It took some explaining for me to understand that that was the name of the dish.

Andrew and I did figure out there was a machine down the hall that would make your food hot in less than one minute, so we got cans of beans to nuke before bed. Our bodies wanted to be full so we could sleep. In South Sudan I loved tomatoes and we ate lots of them, so someone brought me tomato juice to drink as a snack. I have to tell you, "There is not too much I do not like, as I am so thankful for all this food, but, Yucky!"

As weeks turned to months in the States, God provided me with new families of many people with the same goals and ideas of changing the world for the glory of Christ and wanted to see Him lifted up in all the earth. I attended the First Baptist Church of Wadley, where Pastor Skipper led the congregation. What a sweet, small church family.

Yancy taking me for a ride on his motorcycle

A family in Auburn, Alabama, Yancy and his wife Joy, took me into their family. I became so close to them and their immediate family. Our first meeting was in 2006, while being hosted at their house for dinner. Yancy and I took off for a wild motorcycle ride and we became brothers, quickly. Each time we come together we have one thing in common, "We are going to do what they say we can not do." Do you remember that movie? We do not mean this in a bad way, but we are going to change the world for Christ, and why not? Yancy was too quick to influence me in the state of Alabama culture of football; I cannot believe he even took me to an Auburn University game, which I regret now after becoming an Alabama Roll Tide fan.

Have I told you that I love to build a fire and sit near it and how much comfort and fun it offers me? Paul and his wife Christy are very genuine people full of compassion towards others. They live in Wadley, Alabama, on a large area of land. One fall afternoon, Paul had some yard work for Andrew and I to do at his house. This was the first big language barrier and understanding directions problem I encountered. There are so many pine trees on this piece of land and he wanted us to pick up pinecones and put them in a pile. First, I did not know what a pinecone was and there was no way I going to ask. We collected sticks and limbs and a few pinecones for hours. When Paul arrived back to the house, pinecones were still everywhere. Andrew and I were standing proud for all we had done and Paul was looking at us with a big ole question mark.

Needless to say, we had to start over, but we sure know what a pinecone is now and we sang a song with each other, "picking up pinecones, putting em in your pocket" and laughed all the time. Andrew and I built the University of South Sudan in their backyard. We met Paul on one of his short-term mission trips to South Sudan. The team came to love, encourage, and pray with fellow Christians in my country. He witnessed first hand the importance of building a fire and learning from the elders. This fire ring with a South Sudan flag has drawn people from across Wadley to join us for coffee and to enjoy good times with others.

Mr. Jim H. and his family came to the University of South Sudan and we talked and shared many conversations. One day our discussions turned to hunting. Jim asked me if I wanted to go hunting in Alabama. My first thought was, "Hunting with a gun?" I really don't care for guns; I need a bow and arrow or a spear. I shared my nervousness with Jim, which led to practicing how to shoot a gun. Paul and

Chapter Ten - More Studies

Jim convinced me to shoot my first gun. That evening I went to Jim's farm with his boys and I killed my first deer. This was really cool, but it took much courage and help from friends to conquer one of my fears. Seeing a gun during my childhood meant extreme danger and I wanted to stay as far away as possible. This was real life for me and all my Sudanese buddies: war, guns, bombs, and killing. God picked this life for me and He helped me overcome all the difficulties in my life to this point.

Speaking of deer, I was traveling with a friend coming from Dadeville, and it was night and this deer came out of nowhere and jumped so high on the road it knocked the car in its rear panel. I was crying JESUS!!!!!!!!!! Help us! and my friend was worried and scared at the same time. We both looked at each other and did not know what had happened to the car. Is it damaged badly or what? I started praying in the car and when we reached Wadley, I told him to stop so that we could look at the car. We looked the car all over and saw nothing damaged, but oh, we saw the blood of that deer everywhere. So we thanked God together for keeping us from having a wreck.

You know, I have never worn a coat on a daily basis running in the heat of South Sudan. I received this heavy rainproof jacket with a zip out liner and a hood. My mind was thinking, what in the world am I going to do with this and it is taking up so much room in my closet. I found out really quickly as fall and winter approached that this was a warm blessing to cover me during the cold weather.

Adjusting

It was early November and I had been adjusting very well but it was very cold and windy outside. I had a very good sleep the night before and when I woke up before I did anything, I prayed and called my grandfather. He was getting very old and when I said hello to him and I asked him, "BABA, where are you and what are you doing?" He said, "I am in my garden collecting my grand nuts three miles away from the house." I said, "Baba you are old, you do not need to do all this. I wish I was there to help you." He said, "No, I am fine and do you know how happy I am for you because you are studying? When you come back here, I will not work but you can do all for me. I am praying for you and all of your friends in US." I said, "Thank you, Baba, for taking care of me during the time of war. You became like a mother and like a father to me, but above all you told me about Christ and you led me to the cross of Jesus where we get victory over everything. Praise be to God."

Today, I am very happy because I have talked to my grandfather and I have heard his voice. Americans love to have activities going on all the time. They are very active in everything and love to keep it going. There are always weather changes; summer is so hot you can't breathe and the air is still, or fall with the crisp breezes and changing leaves. Winter brings cold freezing weather and possibly snow, or spring with rain, thunderstorms, and tornados. My body has had to adjust and about the time it does, the weather changes again.

Americans love their sports - this can be football, basketball, baseball, soccer, golf, Nascar racing, hunting, or fishing. These hobbies are important "do or die" events, especially in Alabama. Sports are discussed in the classroom, at social gatherings, in family evenings, or even in the church during Sunday school. A friend told me that if you want to talk to someone who you don't know in the South, bring up sports and you are in the discussion.

The English language has always been a second language for me, but it was British style. I thought of myself as someone who knew fairly well how to speak this language prior to coming to college. I had no idea there were so many words that meant the same exact thing or some had the exact pronunciation yet mean something totally different. I mean, think about me trying to pass English class with sentences like, "He could lead if he would get the lead out." Or how about, "The farm was used to produce produce" or "There is no time like the present, therefore, he thought it was time to present the present." My mind was scrambled, just like my eggs.

In Alabama, the Deep South, there are even more sayings, words, and Southernisms that still puzzle and confuse me, but I have learned to interpret lots of them. One night, I went on an errand with my mom and she was gone inside the store for longer than I had expected. When she returned to the car she said, "I'm so sorry. I ran into an old friend and she can talk the ears off a billy goat." I belly laughed and laughed at this saying. Since learning this, I have met many people who have billy goat ears. Some more funny sayings to me include, "Heavens to Murgatroyd" and "scoot over". What in the world is the meaning of these phrases? I also got a big laugh out of my friends when my "pants were too young, my eyes were expired, and next tomorrow was my appointment."

I have also attended the school of nicknames. I figured out that grandparents all have nicknames, not just grandmother and grandfather. There are lots of names under the sun, like: Honey, Granny, Sweets, Shug, Mister, Pawpaw, Jojo, and Buster. I am always chilly or cold, therefore, I inherited the name "snowman". One of my friends looks like a video game character, his nickname is "Wii"; our cars were nicknamed "the squirrel"and "turtle" and "the pearl"; hot sauce is called "yellowjacket". In South Sudan we do not use the word "cousins". We call them brothers and sisters. Can I tell you how confusing this is when I tell a story about my brother, but everyone thought they were all deceased? It took forever to get this straight. Man, this English language can be grueling.

Back in 2006, when we visited the United States, one of our 37 cities was Birmingham, Alabama. There our team met with the Mitchells and others for dinner at a place called Dreamland BBQ. This evening our lives connected and from this point onward, I became part of their family. It sounds very strange how a short meal can change a family forever, but sometimes God coordinates things that we don't understand. All of us knew in our hearts that we would be able to acknowledge that He is working His plan for His glory.

While in school at SUSCC, the Mitchells

would come and take Andrew and I to Birmingham for the weekend or holidays. One special weekend I was picked up early Friday and taken to Birmingham to attend an event called Secret Church led by Dr. David Platt. I recall in my mind the week I spent with him in South Sudan. David came to my village in 2004, and taught us from the book of Romans, which was amazing. We had tea together around the fire and shared our hearts about reaching the nations for Christ. David was a great teacher and what a great joy to hear him again after so many years. After Secret Church, we arrived back at our house around 1am, and I thought, "It was great to study and learn about the Holy Spirit".

The following morning, I was inducted into this crazy American family. Lisa got up early and ran to our beds to pull the blankets off our heads or pull our toes. I was stunned and began to kick and unwrap myself from the four blankets covering me. I was freezing in this house. It seemed like forever to find my way from under the covers and figure out what in the world was going on. This was not fun for someone who loves to sleep in during the weekends. Yes, I love my sleep in America! It is such a safe and deep sleep. I described to her that as a child I did not enjoy sleep in the forest because I might have to run, or it might rain, or mosquitos might be gnawing at me, and many other distractions. Now I want to rest as much as I can, so please do not show up in my room. Well guess what? She came anyway to wake me up and we all laughed, joked and were happy.

Today was a day of lessons, but I had no idea what the lesson would be. After breakfast it was time

Chapter Ten - More Studies

for a "take care of yourself" lesson. I was taken to the sink in the bathroom with my new toiletry caddy in hand. The first lesson was the face scrub with a buff puff. I was told it would be a little rough on my skin but would clear up acne in a couple of weeks."What is acne? How do you spell that?"

Next, Crest on the spinning toothbrush. I was shown how to get every tooth, top and bottom, but I felt the need to spit this paste and foam out. At one point, I was brushing my tongue with the revolving head and laughing and making a big mess. Next, Listerine! with instructions DO NOT SWALLOW - put a swig in your mouth, swish and then spit it out. "How much is a swig?" I had no idea. I turned up the bottle and filled my mouth. SPIT it out! My mouth was wide open and my tongue was stuck out like it was on fire. Hot and stinging, this will get the germs out of my mouth. Moving on to oil-free lotion for my face and Visine for my eyes. "How in the world do you place these drops in your eyes?" Burn and blink, I couldn't see.

Next in the bucket was something called astringent. I was instructed to drip some on the end of a cotton swab and clean my ears. I already knew about a cotton swab and how to use them. After all this, I repeated the instruction to make sure I didn't use one of these products in the wrong area, like swish the astringent or Listerine my eyes. This lesson ended with discussions about anti-bacterial soap killing germs, shampoo for your hair, shaving cream and razor for your face and when to change the blade.

I tell this story for one reason -- Americans are

so blessed and take so much for granted. In South Sudan, I had no idea any of these things existed. Here, you not only have running water, electricity and food, you even have hygiene products. This same weekend, I received my first laptop computer of my very own and I learned how to use Skpe and Facebook. I am learning so much on a daily basis and I am beyond blessed and oh so grateful. Thank You Father for allowing me to see and share these blessings, too.

Getting Out

It's right before the December holiday and after a long day of school, travel from Wadley and a meeting with a mission team going to my country, I arrived at the Mitchell's house for a one week visit. Andrew and I were promised that we would get to drive a car this week in a big empty parking lot. Although it was late, Rick, Lisa, Spencer, me, and Andrew headed for Spain Park in Spencer's giant white Avalanche truck. After lessons about the keys, gears, brakes, steering wheel, et cetera, Andrew wanted to go first. "I'm getting OUT!" I shout while he was driving. "I do not want to be in this moving vehicle with him at the control." Everyone was laughing so hard (except Andrew) as I opened the door and bailed out to the grass area.

Sure enough, Andrew hit the concrete curb. Finally, it was my turn and I was glad I did not hit anything. My hands gripped the steering wheel until they turned white, but I was not sure how hard to push the gas pedal. I think the truck really just coasted. The feeling of being behind the controls of a vehicle is one where you have to think of many things at one time and it was different than I had imagined. God continues to open more doors for me, and He keeps doing great things for me. I am so thankful to Him for everything and all that is yet to come.

First Christmas

This is my first Christmas in the States and the traditions here are very different than ours in South Sudan. Imagine that! Things like Santa Claus coming to town, Christmas trees, fruitcake, lights hanging on trees and houses, many events and giving gifts to one another.

Ours is a Christmas day of going to church, singing songs, praying, going to play games in the field, and giving food to friends. Above all things, what I know and see is that we live in different places and have different cultures, but it is all about the birth of our Lord Jesus Christ. To God be the glory and on earth let there be peace for those who love the Lord. I always thank God for Jesus who came to save us and to set all of us free from the power of sin. Jesus, whom we celebrate is no longer a baby, but is King and is seated at the right hand of God Almighty. To Him be all the glory and power forever and ever. Amen.

Christmas in the States is celebrated very differently from where I was raised. Lisa asked me, "What would you like Santa Claus to bring you for Christmas?" I responded, "Who is this guy? Is he from Alabama?" She started to chuckle and kept going on and on. "Why is this funny? I do not know this man, so why would I ask him to bring me something?" This thought makes me ask even more questions, "Have I met this guy before?" Lisa told me he was from the North Pole and he comes every Christmas Eve to visit children around the world, riding in a sleigh, pulled by eight reindeer. None of this is making any sense at all. Santa Claus showed up at our house in a bright red suit and hat, a bushy white beard and black boots saying, "HoHoHo." I was finally educated on what all of this means. I can tell you, this is a true example of how multicultural families can function. South Sudan does not have any such a thing as Santa Claus or fairy tales. For our Christmas, we go to church, mostly under the tree, to worship God for sending us a Savior. However, gifts are exchanged among family members and much food is prepared to eat, hot tea is served, and coffee too. Several different games are played and those who win will be given a gift. Villages come together to compete and participate in the games. This is how Christmas was celebrated in South Sudan. Family is very important in one's life and the old saying goes, "Your story begins at home and it ends at home". I am more than blessed to have a family in South Sudan and many people that God has brought my way in the States. I have so much more to learn and my American families have given me love and hope in the times I have needed encouragement.

It's Just a Game

One thing we did not do as a family in South Sudan is watch football because we do not have TV. We are running for our lives on any given day. I cannot describe how appreciative I am for my American father, who taught me the meaning of delay of game, first down, flag down, and touch down! Rick, whom I call Pal, told me many times that even if our team loses, we need to understand that Christ always wins and He will not lose!

My Sweet Baba

I was on phone with Baba to wish him a happy holiday and I was talking with him about the weather here in Alabama. He was worried about me because he knows it is hard for me when it is cold. "How will you survive there?" I explained to him that I have warm clothes and a coat to put on and I will be fine. I told him it was also raining in Alabama. Baba said, "Is it like our rain here or there is no water when it is raining there?" I laughed at him and told Baba, "Yes, there is water here just like South Sudan." This is a great demonstration of how our words can be miscommunicated due to our language translation. He was so happy and we continued talking. All of a sudden in the middle of our conversation, Baba said, "Now my tea is getting cold and let us stop here because I want to take my tea." and so I said, "Baba, you do not want or need me now? You said you want your tea." My sweet Baba said, "I miss you my son and we have great fun together."

January brought the second semester of school with more learning and more language barriers to overcome. English 101 and American History consumed most of my time, but new relationships were forming with college friends. The community and those I met in 2006, continued to support me physically, mentally, and financially, but the cost of college was increasing. I prayed and fasted for God's will to be done and His hand to lead me in my education as I completed my first year of college in America.

The date of July 4th in America is a big day, where everyone goes at night to see fireworks. My dear friends, Mark, Sherri, and their family invited me to spend Independence Day weekend with them. We had so much fun playing different types of games and eating foods of all kinds. This little barrel was making a grinding noise as it spun around and around with ice and rock salt. I had no idea the best food of all would come out: Homemade Ice Cream. I just kept eating and eating more. I don't know how many times I went back for more.

After a full day of pleasure, Mark invited me to join them in downtown Birmingham to see the fireworks. I was so excited about this because I love to build a fire to sit around it with friends, but I could not imagine what it would be like in America. On our way the traffic was so heavy and I thought to myself we are going to miss this building of the fire. After growing old in the traffic jam, we arrived, but I didn't see any fire. I didn't see any firewood or a place to make a fire. I started to question my

Chapter Ten - More Studies

English interpretation of this event. Mark explained to me how the show was going to play out and I was thinking okay, "No problem." A few minutes later, the first burst exploded into the sky and I froze in my seat and closed my eyes. It never crossed my mind that there were going to be sounds like those when my village was under attack. I could barely hear the ooooz and ahhhhs from those around me, as I was trembling inside and my mind was racing with traumatic thoughts. Mark's kind heart and love for me noticed how uncomfortable and upset I was feeling, and he took me away from this place. All the bad memories had come to the front of my brain and physically I was in America, but my mind was in South Sudan.

Chapter Eleven - Faith and Family

The faith family at The Church at Brook Hills in Birmingham has stood by me in prayers and welcomed me with open arms into the church. Guess who is the senior pastor of this church? Dr. David Platt, my friend and missionary, who visited my Moruland in 2004. We challenged one another to reach the nations for Christ. God has a plan and He unfolds it little by little each and every day.

The Three-Sixty Birmingham ministry, led by Chad G. interviewed and accepted me into their education program for two years. I transferred from Southern Union State Community College to Jefferson State Community College in Birmingham, Alabama, where I studied and completed my Associate's Degree in Communications. Three-Sixty provided my every need and my education expenses. This ministry worked hard to teach me life skills that will last a lifetime. For all those who have contributed toward my schooling, I can never repay you or thank you enough. This ministry's objective was to bring total change and transformation to the lives of young men by bringing a Godly group of men to mentor and to pray with one another on a daily basis. This program was more than just school or education, they invested their lives and it was the best gift anyone could ever give. Relationships were built that will last for eternity. I will never be in this environment again, but I have best friends forevermore.

In August 2009, four young men, including myself, became the inaugural class and moved in with our houseparent's, Rick and Lisa, near JSCC. Three-Sixty ministry prayed, searched, and interviewed families looking to pour their lives into young men from South Sudan and Inner-city Birmingham. The Mitchell's obeyed God's call to help, and so applied for the task and opened their home to become a global household. Stephen, Jerime, Andrew, and I were all very reserved in our personalities the first few weeks. There were so many new learning experiences, as well as a new school, new home, new friends, new roommates, new church, new chores, and new parents. It is amazing to see how God created people all the same, yet so different. It was not easy with many cultures and habits happening at the same time. Things could go wrong quickly, but our family was the most fabulous on the globe.

During football season, every week we got ready for the game and we all said "May the best team win." We could cheer our team, jump, yell, tease each other, and do all the things that boys love. By the way, are were six boys in the house with Mama Lisa as the only girl, and Blair, our little dog, who would cheer with us. We all grew together as a team and have a bond that will never be broken.

Sometimes we would get mad with each other, but we forgave and loved each other more. After all the fun, Rick brought his Bible out for devotion and prayers from the Word of God. He reminds me of my grandfather, who did not miss a day of reading the Word of God. Those are the moments we all love and cherish. One of the best and most fun ideas was when we were reading through the Bible from Genesis to Revelation and we used a book called Operation World. This book had a different country pray for each day and it gave us the religious statistics and needs for that country. This gave us an opportunity to pray for the Nations of the world together.

I want to tell you a little bit about my American mom, dad, and brothers. I am the middle child, which is the best for me. Wesley is always smart and thinks with critical analysis. I trust him to tell me what is the best way to do things right the first time. I love him so dearly and his nickname is "Wiseman". This is a direct interpretation from a Moru word to English and the term fits him perfectly. Wesley is a few months older than me and I can tell you he is a wonderful young man. He is a man of character, integrity, and honor and I hope my children will be like Wiseman when they grow up. He is a man of little words, quick in action, very compassionate, and loves to help others in anyway possible. On the other side of me is Spencer, who is our younger brother. He is always ready to help others, anytime, or anywhere. "Boom," is his nickname, and he puts others first with no worry about himself, just like my grandfather. Spencer and I met back in 2006, and became friends, instantly. He always inquires about where I am and how life is treating me. Spencer is the funny brother and always makes us belly laugh. I fondly remember him sending emails to me and asking mom to call ITAM to know my whereabouts in the States. Spencer has a heart to love others; he has been in many countries sharing the love of Christ by working in slums and orphanages in South and Central America. I learned most of my American culture and language from the Mitchells and I am still learning even today. Our family has many expressions and sayings we use to communicate with one another. We all know the exact meaning or what the other one needs. It's kind of like our own tribal language from the Mitchell house.

"Lala," is Lisa's nickname, and she is one of the happiest mothers, and she has children from South Sudan, Ethiopia, Inner-city Birmingham, and Choctaw County, Alabama, as well as her own two boys. She loves each of us and is the best mother of all time. Rick, my American father, is always gracious, humble, and full of wisdom. He works hard always and lives the example for all of us. He is not a man of too many words, but rather a man of action. He hates inaction and is always ready to do or to be a part of everything in our lives. I remember having chores assigned for each of us, and we always found Rick doing what we were supposed to be doing. We would tell him to go and rest and he would never do that at all. His friendship with each of us is built strong and good, and so with the bad or indifferent, we can always be ourselves.

Global parenting is the picture of a happy family and I praise God for having them in my life.

Chapter Eleven - Faith and Family

Living life with a family, instead of in a dorm, helped me to learn many things I needed to understand in American culture. How could I know about the differences if I am unable to see it every day? They showed me what Thanksgiving looks like in USA, as we all gathered to eat delicious and well-done turkey. I learned it takes a long time for the preparation of this meal. I know because I had cooking duty in the Three-Sixty program during this week. It changes one's way of thinking about how important it is to get together and give thanks with one's family.

Growing up I used roots for washing my clothes at the nearest creek, but when I got to the States, Lisa gave me lessons on how to wash my clothes with a machine. My clothes smelled so clean and fresh. One thing I learned growing up in Africa is how to iron my clothes before wearing them. Baba and I had an old metal iron and hot charcoal pieces are inserted in the base to make it hot. On this side of the world, the iron has many different settings and gets really hot. A fold out board is available just for ironing and there is a spray that makes my clothes with no wrinkles. One time, I ironed everything including my underclothes and socks.

Looking back at the way I accomplished tasks is so funny now and I laugh at myself. Especiallly watching the movie about the Lost Boys of Sudan, it was hilarious to watch these men. I could see myself doing the exact actions. The movie was my story, it was my life, but because of new knowledge, my future more promising and therefore much different. Someone, somewhere took courage and stood with me, wanting to show me the love of Christ with a promise and a great future. That love is all about God loving each of us by sending His Son to change our lives, and friends, it doesn't get any better than that.

Shortly after joining Three-Sixty, I began designing crosses out of any kind of material available to me. I used tin, metal, wire of all gauges, beads, glass, wood, plastic, old jewelry, cardboard and clay to name a few. I began selling the crosses to friends, and then moved to attending craft shows and taking them to churches and speaking engagements. The design in my mind has changed numerous times as I continue to put them together. This money has given me some spending dollars as well as helped me provide food and school for my mom and half-brother.

The Caldwell family has had a tremendous impact on my life. Their young couple advice and biblical counsel has helped me to see a perspective on issues I would not have known otherwise. Staci has spent hundreds of hours traveling and working at craft shows to sell my handmade crosses to help me raise money for my education and family in South Sudan. She has worked behind the scenes determined to see that I succeed in my endeavors. Selling and making crosses may sound silly, but I can tell you God has blessed me beyond measure. Thank you God for the True Cross that has given hope to all of us.

Throughout Birmingham, God has blessed me with great people who have prayed with me and encouraged me in the difficult times. Among these great friends are the Morsons and Uptons. What a joy to know and spend time with this large family. I will never forget the day I worked at their house and on the ride home, driving on I-65 south, Mr. Morson began to pray for me in tears. After the amen, he looked at me and said, "Bullen, we serve a faithful God and all the plans that He has for you and me will come to completion one day. Let us rest in His promises". This is etched in my brain.

One of my best friends, Jonathan S., who encouraged me during my school struggles and studied with me until the wee hours, made an everlasting impact on my life. I was met with so much trouble in math class and for the life of me I could not understand it. My Jordanian friend was so determined to help me through this class that he met with my teacher to get exact instructions for me to learn in order to pass. Jonathan did this for me in between his classes, homework, and job. What a friend! What a sacrifice!

All the Three-Sixty board members, volunteers, and tutors walked these two years at JSCC with me and I am so humbled by your love for me. The Precept small group, Donna, Butch, Robyn, Brenda, Martha, Janice, and others, who came to the house week after week for Bible study, became a huge part of my life. My college friends and I studied "Covenant" alongside this group and what a clear picture of how God's covenant is woven from Genesis to Revelation. They became part of my journey and supported my studies through financial contributions, prayers, and words of encouragement. Robyn and her sweet mom, Paula, took the radical challenge and their whole family joined in helping my brother, Paul, in Africa, and also me.

God has blessed me with many other gracious people too, including the Quinns, Spears, Pughs, Bickels, and Frosts, as well as my dear friend Sandra P. I could go on and on naming the individuals who have invested in my life and my education on an ongoing basis. We all need people who we can talk to about situations in life and not all friends are alike. Some of them are funny, some are very serious, and some just do not know what they can do to help but their presence, prayers, and hugs are so important. All I can say is that I am very grateful and forever will be for all that each of you has done in my life.

In early 2011, as I was completing my Associate's Degree in Communication at Jefferson State Community College, suddenly and out of nowhere, the Three-Sixty board of directors announced that at the end of this semester, the ministry would be closing. I was informed that I would be returning to Africa at this time. Shocked and confused as to the problem, I prayed that God would show me His plan and direction. I knew in my mind that God had placed this desire for an education in my heart and that He had provided every single detail. While continuing to study and pass exams during that semester, God was at work. Four Corners Ministries contacted me about partnering with them to raise the money needed to complete my degree. I applied and was accepted to transfer to Troy University. I am so humbled and blown away by this journey. God has brought me through each day with the body of Christ and individuals praying and supporting me. Today, we are raising the stone to remind me of the goodness and faithfulness of our God, who reigns forever.

I have never dreamed that one day I would be in America going to vote for the future of my own country. This week South Sudanese are traveling and walking miles to vote for independence. God is so good in all His ways and has given us the time to decide for the future to become the 193rd country in the world.

I had to travel to Nashville, Tennessee, which was the appointed voting place in the United States. As I was standing in this long line to vote, my mind replayed all that has happened to my family and me during the many many years of war in Sudan. I feel tears streaming from my eyes and down my face. I lost much of my family to this war, but thanks to God, I am alive to vote for the future generations.

Hopefully, they will not have to walk through the paths that I have walked. Therefore, hope is not seen sometimes in the beginning but it is in the end. Keep your dreams and hope alive. This is a great thing to do because one day it will come true.

One of my longtime friends told me about a "fork in the road". At the fork there are different directions to travel. For me, it is a "road on the fork" because Christ is the road or the way according to scripture. He has overcome all, and we, who trust in Him will never be victims but victorious. Bring up the challenge and let the games begin. I can assure you, that if Christ is your captain, the victory has already been won many years ago. Rest in Him and worship in Victory, rejoice in Victory and walk in Victory.

Chapter Twelve - Associates to Bachelor

The summer of 2011, was a big ole sweatshop. I worked my fingers to the bone making and designing crosses to raise money for my school. I traveled to many different churches and organizations, sharing my story. I worked any job available including cutting grass, cleaning garages, or moving items. God provided so many people to help me during this process. In a very busy three short months, God gave me the desires of my heart and helped me raise enough money to attend Troy University. Like many other people, I did not want other people to know my needs and I despised asking others to help me. I believe that God wants us to work. This was so important that I have money for my upcoming semester of school.

Four Corners Ministries was my sponsoring organization, but I was responsible for raising the funds needed to attend school. If we would remember what happened in the book of Genesis, we would be excited to work because there are no more free rides. Adam and Eve messed it up and we all have to work in order to provide for ourselves. That is why I am excited about my education and how God is going to use it for the expansion of His Kingdom. I cannot begin to tell you how many times I have been lacking funds for tuition, food, housing, Internet, phone, haircuts, toiletries, et cetera, and every single time, God has provided! But I was prepared for whatever God had in store for me and I kept going, counting it all joy. Life is a journey and if you stop, you go nowhere. All praise and honor goes to God for my education and to the people who

He has used to help me get to the next chapter of His plan.

I moved to Troy University ready to finish a Bachelor's degree in Communications. Once again, here I was in a new city, at a new college and I did not know anyone. The campus is so nice with flowers and fountains. I was assigned to live in Alumni Hall and it was the oldest building on campus. The room was acceptable, but the bathroom was another story. Needless to say, I used some of my tuition dollars to purchase shower shoes when I found booboo in the shower stall. The international students at Troy are from sixty-seven different countries. God continues to bless and give me opportunities to share His love and the gospel with other students.

After meeting with my advisor, I was informed of many differences in the Communication's degree at Troy verses JSCC and I had to change my major to Business. This added at least six more classes to my schedule, which included high level math classes, statistics, and accounting. Oh boy! Hard work, long nights, tutors, deep breaths, more tuition, and faith in Him who knows my strengths and weaknesses got me through each class, one at a time.

A member of The Church at Brook Hills, Riley heard about my story and my enrollment at Troy University. He was from the Troy, Alabama, area and connected me with friends and a church in the area. Rob who was the pastor at Covenant Grace, and his family, welcomed me with open arms and were there to help me in anyway at all. Rhett was a member at this new church plant and he was also an instructor at Troy University. He and his wife, Donna, supported me through prayers, love, and encouragement when I needed it the most. I was also blessed with another brother in Christ, Bryant and his family, who were a joy for me to have in my life. They helped make my life easy and shared with me their children, fellowship, and family. We had all the fun under heaven. Matt, Gwen, and many other members of my new church family encouraged me, supported me, and stood with me till I finished my studies. God brought this sweet congregation into my life and used each member to help me with transportation, grocery shopping, tutors, love, and prayers. Thank you Covenant Grace.

The majority of this first year at Troy University was spent with my nose in a book. One weekend, Andrew and I were invited to speak at a church in Hornlake, Mississippi. A youth group spent the weekend learning about the lives of persecuted Christians. We were locked in a jail cell for hours as we roll played for these students what it looks like to be persecuted for your faith in Jesus Christ. It was a wonderful eye-opening weekend as we worshipped God together, and I am so thankful for this opportunity.

My final year at Troy was spent going to school every day, all day, including summer, taking as many hours as I could squeeze into my schedule. I studied day and night and night and day with very little extra curricular activities. I was determined to finish strong, and God sustained me and was my Strength. During these last semesters, I lived in several different locations on campus; Newman, the BCM, and the Gunter House. The Gunter's were the sweetest couple and they helped many international students with housing, and I was one of their recipients.

Graduation day never felt so good and my heart was full. God has provided this education in His time. I was on cloud nine as I met the Chancellor and prepared to walk. Friends and family gathered to celebrate with me as I accepted my diploma, moved my tassel, and fellowshipped with a meal. As I walked across campus to the party place, I had no idea what was about to happen. The door opened and I saw many friends from all over the state of Alabama, and then my eyes locked in to the face of a very special guest from West Virginia. Beth Grayson, my teacher in Mundri, had traveled to Troy for my special day. What a surprise! What a joy!

Many friends spoke words of encouragement and congratulations as we ate chili and Heavenly donuts. A money tree was standing with lights and sweet cards attached and I had so much fun reading each and every word. As this celebration came to a close, a video began to play on a large movie screen in the front of the room. The tears would not stop flowing as I see and hear from my best friend in

Juba, Charles; then Bishop Bismark; then Rebecca; then my half brother, Paul; then Timothy Keller, from South Africa; and last, my sweet momma; all of them sending their love and excitement. Go Trojans!

Chapter Thirteen - Returning as Missionary

I have been in the United States almost 4 years and would really like to go to Moruland for a visit. I began conversation with Four Corners Ministries, friends and school immigration counselors about the process and possibility of a visit home during the summer of 2012. South Sudan has only been a country for one year and no one is really sure of the process or documents needed to travel. It was a blind leading the blind scenario. The situation currently is that I have a Sudanese passport, which is expired; a Sudanese birth certificate, which is now another country; an F1 student visa from Uganda with five names, and then I need to travel across the ocean to fix all of these issues. I also must raise the money needed for my airplane ticket. As a precaution, I was advised to obtain an emergency travel document by my USCIS officer at Troy, which I did immediately and it arrived promptly.

God had this amazing plan already in motion, unbeknownst to me. Several great role models, businessmen, and dear friends in Birmingham invited me to travel with them on an expedition and they would also go to my homeland with me. Are you kidding? Wow! Do you know how excited I was to take these brothers in Christ to Mundri? Everything fell perfectly into place and I was headed home!

I started this expedition with George Y., who is one of the most influential persons I have ever known. He was my traveling partner from Atlanta to England. In England, we joined Bob Q., one of my role models and a dear friend. Bob has been mentoring me for several years and introduced me to a new, funny friend, Dean S. This strong group of businessmen who have been serving the Lord with their skills, resources, and expertise would make you rethink what it means to be a Christ follower and a businessperson. These fellows have been in "business as a mission" for many years and they have been teaching economic development and microbusiness in Eastern Europe and East African nations. Rejoice and Hope Ministries International has been a blessing for many believers and committed Disciples of Christ in Dar El Salam and the surrounding areas in east Africa.

The four of us flew to Dar El Salam and joined the rest of the team, totaling about twenty-five of us all together. As a team, we headed to the village of Morogoro to serve with a medical and pastors conference. In the evening there was open air preaching, where many folks came to know Christ as their Savior and put their trust in Him for salvation.

Being Faithful with Talent

There is no greater joy than to see people trusting in Christ and becoming His disciple and going to share with others what they have experienced. After a couple days in this village, the four of us came back to Dar El Salaam for a Christian business conference. Hundreds of businessmen and women gathered to hear and learn how to be a faithful servant of Christ in any business. The goal is to make Him known and make Disciples in every market place. The understanding of doing business is misunderstood in many African churches and this conference created many questions from those in attendance. Many believers look at business as something they should not be part of or practice. By the grace of God, we were able to explain how they could conduct their business in a very honest and accountable manner as they serve the Lord with gladness.

Reading directly from the Word of God and explaining the biblical point of view, Dean, a seasoned businessman, taught about marketing. He explained how to use your God-given talent in the business world as you interact with customers on a daily basis. George, who is a business owner, told the story of the widow's oil and Elijah from 1 Kings 17: 8-24. All the widow had was a fist full of flour and a little oil in a jug for her and her son. Elijah, a man of God, told her to make him a small cake of bread so he would have something to eat. He also told her to make some for her and her son. Elijah then said, "The jar of flour will not be used up and the jug of oil will not run dry until the day the Lord gives rain on the land." God used Elijah to teach the widow to use her last resource to bless a total stranger. He taught them to use what they have, even to sell like the widow does to expand the kingdom of God. Bob taught that "God owns everything". Knowing that He owns everything on earth and in heaven then we do not own our businesses. God owns them and He wants to use them for His glory.

I met a young man who was thrown out of his family by this father because he confessed and trusted in Christ. This man told me that he was going back to his tribe to proclaim Christ so that all will know Him as Lord. Assurance like this will blow your mind away, but that is the power of the cross. The conference shared something new to most of those in attendance and it was very eye-opening for many.

> *"For the word of the cross is foolishness to those who are perishing, but to us who are being saved it is the power of God."*
>
> **1 Corninthians 1:18**

Poor and Needy

Changing the World for His Glory

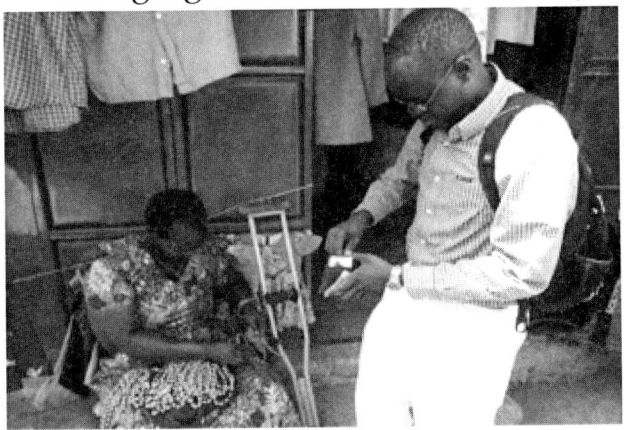

This is not the end of the story, after two weeks in Tanzania we made our way to Northern Uganda. We came to fellowship and encourage our brothers and sisters who were already doing "business as a mission". I will never forget Mama Florence, a disabled widow, with five orphans. Even in her situation she has adopted two more children, is a businesswoman, and is one of the biggest donors in her local church. This Disciple of Christ is ready to go to all villages, tribes, and nations to proclaim the glory of Christ through her business. I listened to her for hours telling how she has been blessed so she can bless others. This left me without words. Her testimony was a blessing to us and encouraged this team that "business as a mission" will have an everlasting impact on many people in underdeveloped counties of the world. After enjoying all the fun times in Tanzania and Uganda, now it is the right time to introduce my friends into reality! Let us go to South Sudan together.

The last time I was home we were still called Sudan, but this time it is South Sudan. How exciting to have our own country after years of suffering and persecution. As the plane touched the dirt runway at home, I could see new things happening in the country. Those who had run for their lives were slowly coming back to their villages to start a new life. Businessmen and women have started to sell their goods along the roadsides. The infrastructure, which was totally destroyed by the long civil war, with hope was rising again among the people of South Sudan.

Home is Where the Story Begins

My mother and sister got up early, cleaned the compound, and then they took a boda-boda ride to the airstrip to wait for me. After waiting for over three hours at the dirt clearing, they heard a small plane in the distance. Out of the sky it landed. My mom watched to see where it would come to a stop.

Guess who was the first person to jump out of the plane? I was already crying tears of joy to see them coming to greet me. Seeing my mother and my sister again was another joy for me and made my friends standby and smile. The last time I had been home was in early 2008, and it had been four long years. We are crazy funny people, who like to talk very fast and make jokes. My mother was already fired up and she kept serving hot tea, coffee, and more food for all four of us. She loves to show her love to others by feeding them and you can see in her eyes and actions that her heart is singing. While we locals were speaking our Moru language, my American friends were just as confused as they could be.

    I know exactly how they felt because I have been in their shoes more than once. My friends got to witness how we interact with all of our hand gestures, speaking very loudly, and laughing all at the same time. The look on their faces told me they knew this guy had missed home and was so glad to see his family. As my old friends and distant relatives came to visit with me, there was one thing

Chapter Thirteen - Returning as a Missionary

every single one of them were saying: "My, you have changed and grown".

We arrived a little later than expected in my homeland and by the time I got my teammates settled and my mama's good food in my belly, it was a little too late to make the walk to see my grandfather. At this time he was in a wheelchair or bedridden because his leg had been injured. My elderly grandfather fell several months ago when he got his leg caught in the rope that holds the goat. Baba just has not been able to recover well.

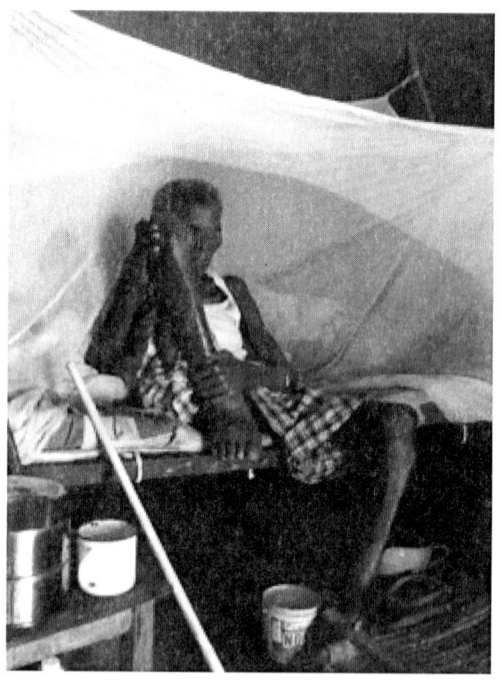

I woke up with the sun to make my way to see my sweet Baba. He knew I was coming to visit South Sudan, but he didn't know the exact date or time. As I began to enter his tukul, I stopped in the doorway and started to sing a song. Baba's weak voice said, "Kuniwa (small rock) is here!!!" That was my grandfather's nickname for me growing up. My Baba was very excited when he heard me singing one of the songs we sang years ago. "Come my boy and let us pray." Oh how sweet the sound to hear his prayers praising Our Father in Heaven. This was another blessed reunion for me and I am thankful God granted this time for both of us before Baba went home to be with the Lord.

While in Mundri, Bob, Dean, and George met with Bishop Bismark, who is the church leader, and he organized the conference with the local businesspersons in the area and some of his church members. We were able to share the same information that we have been teaching throughout the region. The message was meant to encourage business people to be ambassadors for Christ in the market place and make disciples with the talent that God had given to them.

For all those who have trusted in Christ, we are called to global multiplication of Christian discipleship even in our workplace. Doctors can use their talents that were entrusted to them to share Christ at their own offices or on mission trips for the glory of God. Businesspersons, as well, can impart hope to the world and worship God with their talents. One of the most encouraging missions to participate in is to teach and empower local entrepreneurs to conduct holistic business in their small villages or towns. Motivating people to be honest and do well in their small business is going to bring great change for their communities and churches. I also believe this is part of the Protestant work ethic and value system. Creating dependence is one of the challenges we face today in third world countries and we have to be very careful of these situations. We want everyone to put their trust in Christ and depend on Him for every need.

Meeting with Elijah, my new friend from Dar El Salaam, who is a chicken farmer, I could see this man was as motivated and excited as he could be for his business, but that is not the end of his story; he is also a leader of a small group made up of five chicken farmers. He is leading with passion and is full of encouragement towards his fellow farmers, whom he introduced to this type of business and among them there is a widow who had become a successful businesswoman. She was able to pay for her orphaned children's college educations. This widow was determined that she would do all things through Christ who gives her strength.

Business Mission Will Change Africa

These people are Disciples of Christ whose hearts were changed and whose minds have been renewed. They are new creations in Christ and are on mission to change their community for the glory of Christ. Each of them when asked about how successful they have become, are humbled and will point to Christ for what He has done on the cross and the urgency of the gospel to reach the four corners of the earth. Each of them are sharing the gospel with their customers, and inviting unbelievers to see the goodness of the Lord in their businesses. Widows are rejoicing, sinners are coming to Christ; poor people will never be poor again because their dreams are coming true. This is the power of the cross, my friends, to set the captives free and save the sinners from sin. Their mission is to be set free from spiritual and physical poverty. There is a greater respect and love when you teach someone how to "Fish" instead of "giving them a fish". Helping people is something we are all called to do, but are we going to create dependence or are we going to make an investment? Encouraging dependence will cripple one's God given talents and dreams, but investing in people by helping them to become who they are in Christ, and motivating them to work, is holistic, and the result will be glorifying to God.

> *"I know how to get along with humble means, and I also know how to live in prosperity; in any and every circumstance I have learned the secret of being filled and going hungry, both of having abundance and suffering need. I can do all things through Him who strengthens me."*

Philippians 4:12-13

Chapter Fourteen - Appreciation

I would not be where I am today without the LORD, who is my Shepherd and Salvation, my Strong Tower and my Very Present Help in the times of trouble. He has defended me when I was helpless, He has protected me when I needed protection, and He has provided all that I have needed. My Lord is my Comforter and my Hope. I am not perfect in my walk with Him, but His everlasting love and grace are enough for me. It is not an easy road. There are so many challenges and unknowns, but He walks beside me and takes me through the rough terrain of life. All that I have had need of, His great hand has provided. This safari of life is not over yet, but I have assurance that His promise is with me. I do not need to do anything to protect myself or be brave of my own fruition, but He who calls me will finish His work in me.

Graduating from college, with an Associate's Degree in Communications from Jefferson State Community College and a Bachelor's of Science Degree in Business Administration from Troy University, was a challenge beyond words. In the end I can look back and raise my hands up to the heavens and praise the Lord! New hope in life is rising stronger, but the most important action is to make His name known among all nations. I have to thank Him, alone, for how far He has brought me and He is able to do more for His glory. I am not worthy to magnify His glory, but thank Him for the grace, which is His unmerited favor so sinners like me can be called His beloved. He has brought so many people into my life to walk this global journey with me.

Chapter Fourteen - Appreciation

It began with my wonderful and courageous mother who gave birth to her son in her small mud tukul house in the hottest month in South Sudan. My first three years of life had been amazing just like other kids who are born in Africa. Mom and dad provided me parental love and took care of me and I love them with all of my heart, forever. Although that lasted for only three years due to the civil war, God brought my grandfather who became my best friend of all time. He was my role model, a godly man, who seeks nothing from men but depends on Christ for everything in his daily life. Baba was not ashamed of the gospel of Christ and had nothing to boast in but the cross of Jesus. There are so many principles Baba always told me:

- do not talk about yourself, but rather let others be the one's you speak well of

- not too many words should be spoken, but rather to let my actions speak

- do not complain of anything but rather be thankful and rejoice, because this is the day that the Lord has made, and we better be glad

- to look for friendship rather than wasting time and energy in creating conflict.

I could go on and on. Baba's love for the gospel and his passion for serving others were truly amazing.
Baba always would introduce himself as "Ruinduba" which means servant. God has en-

larged my boundaries by bringing men and women of faith into my life. They have walked with me as I have grown. Missionaries from all over the globe have been a major part in helping me get an education. There is no way I would be where I am today without the prayers, support, and encouragement from them. I can't even begin to count the number of friends in the United States who have opened their arms of love to allow me to come and study in one of the best places on this earth where there is peace and freedom.

Therefore, bothers and sisters as I have finished my education in American I am calling you all to join me in this calling to go to South Sudan and other eastern African countries to share the gospel through microbusiness. You can come and teach any business skill and share the gospel with the people who are determined and ready to see a change in their society. You can help us by organizing fundraisers at your house, or through your churches, to help us with the capital that is needed for those brave people whom have nothing with which to start a business. You can sponsor a child, a businessperson, a chicken farmer, or even a goat farmer, whose life will change forever for the glory of God. I know we can do it by the help of our Heavenly Father and our Lord Jesus Christ through the Holy Spirit and to Him be the glory forever, Amen!

> *"And Jesus came up and spoke to them, saying, "All authority has been given to me in heaven and on earth. Go therefore and make disciples of all the nations, baptizing them in the name of the Father and theSon and the Holy Spirit, teaching them to observe all that I commanded you; and lo, I am with you always, to the end of the age."*

Matthew 28:18-20

My studies that began in the jungle under a tree does not end under the tree folks, but it starts again with a college degree from America. Only God can do this! It has been hard, and life is an expedition that has to be walked one day at a time, and it can not be walked alone, as you will have struggles, you will have uncertainies, you will encounter disappointments. God has opened my eyes by His everlasting love and grace to see Him and to trust in Him alone. When God changed my heart, I found peace in Him. Thank you Lord for all that You have done for me! Thank You for my brothers and sisters in Christ that You placed in my life to help me. I am forever grateful for the work of missionaries in Moruland. They have done a remarkable work of Christ throughout the world and I am so thankful for their obedience to the call to go and to make disciples of all nations. God used each missionary to give me the opportunity to have an education and to have the knowledge of today. There are so many who have touched my life without knowing the impact. It is my prayer that I will be a blessing to others and hopefully change one life at a time.

Why Not?

> *"Then Samuel took a stone and set it between Mizpah and Shen, and named it Ebenezer, saying, "Thus far the LORD has helped us."*
>
> **1 Samuel 7:12.**

I am sure when Samuel called all the people of Israel to commemorate the goodness and faithfulness of God, everyone recalled all the things that had happened in their lives and gave praises to God for His faithfulness and goodness. The same goes in our own lives, with every achievement, which one is of our own effort? It is God's gift for us to celebrate and glorify Him for making it possible for us.